AF481494

# LESSONS

## FROM THE MOUNTAINS

by Chris Dahl

Copyright 2020 Chris Dahl

Printed in the U.S.A.

No part of this book, other than a brief excerpt for reviews, may be reprinted without the express written consent of the publishers.

Published by:

Dahl Publishing

P. O. Box 384

Drummond, Montana 59832

dahl@blackfoot.net

Dedicated to my lovely wife Kim—the wife of my youth, my lover, the mother of my kids, the spoiler of my grandkids, my best friend, and my partner in adventure.

# TABLE OF CONTENTS

# PREFACE

In January of 1992, I was in Salt Lake City for the annual sales meeting for Dixon Paper Company, the company which employed me. After a day and a half of workshops and speakers, a line of black stretch limousines picked us up at the hotel and drove us to a country club for the awards banquet. The meal and accommodations provided that evening can only be described as world class. In recognition of my efforts from the previous year, I was awarded an all-expense paid trip to Hawaii for my wife and me, one of only a handful of salesmen from our entire region so honored. In the same hour that I received my award, a florist knocked on the front door of my home back in Helena, Montana and gave my wife a congratulatory bouquet of flowers, compliments of the company. Later that night, in my private room at the Little America Hotel, I found myself inexplicably restless. Almost completely full and yet somehow half empty, as if I couldn't help but enjoy the symptoms of this new-found luxury but almost instinctively afraid of the disease. In the wee hours I penned the following essay:

## THE PAVEMENT OR THE MOUNTAIN

I have been about learning the craft of salesmanship. With purpose and intent, I now walk the tiled floors of businesses where my products are being bought. I put coins into the parking meters on the street. I send documents through the air to those who need them and I smile at people I don't especially like. I have been trained to exact my gain in these ways and from these places. Places connected by lots of pavement.

There was a time when this was all exciting and new, learning of men and business and things. To finally be exposed to dollars and success, to be thrust into the arena of the wing-tipped gladiators. I have survived out there on the cutting edge and have met in some degree that definition of success. But it has come at a price. The exposure has been great, and it began to numb me without me even knowing it.

Each year the world turns a little faster and more people demand more things. More days go whirlwinding into oblivion without regard except to goals and appointments. And always the miles and miles and the hours and hours of pavement.

In the quiet, reflective moments of my life my mind's eye would see the deserving woman and the three spunky, blonde-headed kids that share my home and I'd ask myself the questions they didn't know to ask. Which is better, to teach a boy grit or to teach him how to make lots of money? What does a little girl need most, a brand new trampoline or an old dog to take care of? And should my wife's reward be a fat checkbook and a fat husband?

Earlier in life I tested other trails far away from the pavement. I've lived where the night is truly dark and I've had animals to feed. I've seen the sun set on the Sawtooths and seen it rise over the Tetons. I've witnessed the execution of the food chain. I've sat chilled on a ridgetop listening to the silence of morning. I've bathed in lakes above timberline. I've followed and killed deer and elk, and by consuming them completed the mysterious and divine web of the natural order. I've sat on a mountain's top in complete peace and solitude without being lonely, and I've shrunk in fear from a fierce lightning storm thundering across the sky. I've felt many feelings, seen many sights, thought many thoughts, and learned many lessons far away from the pavement.

Perhaps a boy needs grit, but he also needs a new bicycle. A little girl needs a dog, but she also needs an Easter dress. A deserving wife needs a decent and capable husband, but she should also have a decent and capable house. So, somehow, I become a part of the pavement when it links me to the bicycles and the dresses and the couches and curtains, much like I somehow become part of the mountain when I eat the venison from a wild elk.

Which, then, have I become more of? The pavement or the mountain? I fear that this becomes the question that divides. The pavement or the mountain? The grit or the bike? The dog or the dress? The wonderful house or the wonderful husband?

Voices tell me I can have both. All the grit and all the new bikes. The dogs and the dresses. I've striven for all of both, but each year the world turns a little faster, I'm exposed a little greater, and I become a little more numb. The pavement wants my blood. The mountain asks for my heart. Earlier in life I gave the mountain my heart. More recently I've given the pavement my blood. The mortal limits of my life will soon demand a crossroads. Which is the appropriate sacrifice?

Much like the poet Robert Frost, I wish to take the road less traveled by. Give me the grit and the dog. Someday, fully aware of the consequences, I'll take off my wing-tips and leave the pavement for a quieter, and perhaps bumpier, road. God willing, I won't even look back.

*****

Now those three children plus one more are all grown up and gone, and for nearly 30 years I have wrestled for that balance between the pavement and the mountain. These stories are the lessons of the mountains, and of my struggle to give myself to that quieter and perhaps bumpier road.....

# FILLED

*"For precept must be upon precept, precept upon precept;*
*line upon line, line upon line; here a little,*
*and there a little" Isaiah 28:10*

I sense a flicker of movement ahead in the timber, and my teenaged brain instantly clears the song stuck inside and focuses. My feet stop. My nose elevates slightly for no particular reason. My ears strain and I'm suddenly aware of the gurgling sound of the tiny brooklet across the old mining road. My eyes scan left to right to left without moving my face. My heart, the heart of a predator, crescendos to a rapid and purposeful beat. If I had a long tail, the tip of it would begin twitching back and forth. I pick apart the shadows, the shafts of light, the brush and the trees, looking for an odd spot of color or glint of antler or a horizontal line out of place, anything, trying to morph that one brief flicker into a mule deer buck.

Fully concentrated and fully connected, I process the landscape in front of me without satisfaction. Twenty, thirty, or maybe ninety seconds of focus later I relax a little. Must have been nothing. A squirrel maybe, or a sparrow flitting between trees, or my over-anxious mind playing tricks on itself. I am nineteen years old and this state of alertness, this hunter's focus, has always come to me instinctively and easily, but I have not yet learned to listen to the quiet little voice inside that tells me to wait a moment longer, to trust my instincts, to *slow down*.

I take a single step forward and just as my boot hits the ground I see his pointy face staring back at me, framed by two trees but in plain view about 50 yards out. We simply stare at each other for a second or two, a couple of young bucks unsure of their instincts. He wheels and trots toward the timber, bounding across the tiny creek. As if by magic, the rifle over my shoulder comes to arms, the safety clicks, and the magnified view of the deer's chest wobbles around in the center of the rifle scope. The gun booms. The deer doesn't flinch, but slows to a walk and turns away at an angle. Again the crosshairs find the ribcage of the deer. Again the gun goes off. The deer simply stops and stares. I work the bolt in a panic, trying hard not to believe the obvious, that I am missing him from a scant 50 yards away. Just before I can get him centered in the scope again the deer twists in a tight circle and his hind legs buckle. He sits down awkwardly and flops over. As I watch in amazement through the scope, the buck's legs stiffen and then relax.

There is no one to hear the mighty *YES!* I holler to the Sawtooths. No one to hear the echo. No one to record the orange vested happy dance. Nobody around to photograph the moment of a young hunter and his vanquished prey.

I run to him and heft his head. His eyes are bluing already, and a bloody tongue droops out of his sagging mouth. There is absolutely no remorse, no moment of stricken feelings, no conflict whatsoever. I am the hunter and he the hunted. He is all mine. His smallish antlers have a fork on one side and three points on the other. *A nice little buck,* that's what I knew my father would call him. *A good meat buck.* Yes, by golly, I had myself a good meat buck and, for the first time, I had killed a deer all by myself.

I reload my gun and shoot three evenly spaced shots in the air to alert my brother Jason to come and help. I notice the unused binoculars dangling from my neck. *Crap. I need to remember to use my binoculars.* I knew my father, had he been in my place, would have glued his binoculars to his face and found that deer in the shadows and killed him where he stood. I can't believe I didn't spot him anyway, right there in front of my nose. No matter, he's mine now. Fair and square. I eat the apple and the sandwich out of my pocket, waiting for my brother to show up, and the song stuck in my head returns, a heavy metal AC-DC song.

*Shoot to thrill,*

*Play to kill,*

I loosen my belt and slide off the tools necessary for the next part of my day, a knife and a rope. I'd helped Dad gut several deer, including my very first buck, mostly by holding the legs open and listening to the don'ts. *Don't cut the stomach open, don't forget to cut the diaphragm, don't cut your fingers when you cut the windpipe.* Dad let me work the knife some, but I'd never flown solo.

Forty five minutes later I'm sopped to the shoulders in deer blood and gore. The guts are out all right and it looks pretty good in there. I find two blackish holes about three inches apart inside the chest cavity, both good lung shots, and I wonder how come the deer didn't just drop like a rock. I'd cut into the intestines right off the bat, sending an acrid green stream of deer chew and bile over my boots. I had to turn the buck over twice to get all the connective tissue cut, and when I rinsed my hands in the creek I noticed I'd nicked the side of my index finger. Must have been when I was cutting the windpipe. No matter. It was done now.

My brother never shows up, so I loop the rope over the horns of the buck and start dragging. I was a couple of miles from the pickup, and had to get the deer at least to the big wash in the mining road. I picture in my mind taking him all the way to the truck, properly triumphant and back-slapped and "atta-boyed" and tossing him in the bed of the pickup like a sack of potatoes.

Twenty minutes later, my shoulders are burning and my fingers are killing me from the thin rope. The deer isn't sliding very well over the broken road, and his nose keeps rolling under and serving as a plow. My gun constantly slips off my shoulders, and whichever way I try pulling feels awkward and doesn't quite seem to work. I try packing him over my shoulders. I'd seen a painting of the Pilgrims once and an Indian was packing a deer slung over his shoulders to the Thanksgiving feast. It seemed a manly way to pack a deer. What I got for my trouble was a shampoo of sticky deer blood that dribbled down the back of my neck and soaked my shirt. It's twice as hard anyway. I try carrying him in front of me, how you might carry an injured dog into the vet. No way. I discard any notion of a rose-petal entry, and when I hit the wash two hours later, exhausted and hurting, I dump the deer and go for the truck.

When I finally reach the bend of the road that puts the pickup into view, I can see that my dad and brother are leaning over the fenders, chatting and waiting. My dad's face twists gutshot for an instant when he first sees me, then it softens and my welcome is all I imagined it would be. It hasn't occurred to me that by now I must look like the deer shot me.

The whole story gushes out and there are back-slaps and atta-boys and quite often my dad's eyebrow raises, but he keeps his tongue. When I'm done, they tell me about their day. My brother had evidently worked up the ridge above me all right, but the ridge split and he had gone the other direction and claimed not to have heard my shots. Dad had gone here and there and hadn't seen anything. My friend Dave had also shot a buck and it was also a 2 x 3. His dad, Al, who was also my high school football coach, was up helping him get it to the road. Dave and I were both mere days away from reporting to the Missionary Training Center in Provo, Utah to begin our respective two year church missions. I was headed to Sweden, Dave to Japan. It seemed to be appropriate karma that the two prospective missionaries were the ones who got bucks. We gather in the old Ford and bounce over the mining road, and at the wash Dad swings a wide arc through the sagebrush and backs up to the edge. Dad pulls on his well-worn leather gloves as we walk through the wash to see my deer.

*He's a dandy,* Dad says. *A nice little buck.* He kneels and pats the deer on the front shoulder, as if thanking the flesh and blood answer to a father's silent prayer.

Then Dad straightens out the rope still tied to the buck's antlers and throws a half hitch over the deer's nose, a little trick called a halter hitch. Still chattering back and forth about the events of the morning, Dad breaks a stout stick and ties it to the end of the rope near the deer's nose, grabbing one end and motioning me to the other. With one of us on each side and the halter hitch keeping the deer's nose off the ground, the little buck slides through the wash like a block of ice on a hot floor.

Leather gloves. A halter hitch. A piece of stick, for crying out loud! I didn't say a word and he didn't have to. Later, while the old Ford rumbles toward home and the talk turns to using your binoculars in the timber and hunting the ridges and watching the saddles, I take in all of it, breathing the words in and out with the lingering smell of sage and mule deer blood, absorbing every particle.

A week or so later, our family sits to Mother's dinner of mule deer chops, slow cooked in cream of mushroom gravy, and home-grown baked red potatoes. I eat with purpose, relishing my new and temporary role of provider but, even at nineteen, aware that it is the fat of the land which we eat. It was not me, but Mother Earth that had once again provided, and each bite of that mule deer seemed to magically hold inside it the granite cliffs, the sage and pines, the water and cedars and wild of Alder Creek. These had all combined to provide for the buck, and by extension become a part of me as I chew and swallow.

*You are what you eat.* And at that moment I can't imagine anything better to be than what that buck represented. I had gone as a hunter into the mountains, and with singular purpose and clarity had brought home the meat on my plate.

I eat until I am filled.

*****

After leaving a sales meeting in Billings I buy a resident deer "B" tag, good for an antlerless whitetail. In Montana, a "B" tag is an extra doe tag, a bonus opportunity to put some meat in the freezer and still be able to hunt on an "A" tag, usually good for a buck. "B" tags are a management tool designed to control burgeoning deer populations and keep the landowners, whose crops these deer eat, off the steps of the Fish, Wildlife, and Parks offices. This is a new and exciting proposition for me, one not available in my previous home state of Idaho. Today the road home to Helena will go through Levina, Harlowton, and Two-Dot, and somewhere along the way I hope to find some extra venison for my young family.

West of Harlowton a few miles I spot two beat up ranch pickups pulled into a turnout. I swing my sedan around.

"I've got a doe tag and was wondering if you might know where a guy could pursue some whitetails," I ask.

"You got a tag?" one man asks.

"Yes, sir."

"Well, if you rip that tag into three pieces and shoot a deer for every piece of tag you can hunt on my place. I'm sick of feeding the varmints."

We all laugh and I get directions to his place, including the most likely haystack to sit on. I notice my dashboard clock when I drive past his windbreak. 3:15. Plenty of time to get set up for the evening hunt.

*Varmints.* Somehow the word sits awkward, itchy. Wrong.

I park well before the bluff of the Musselshell River, load my gun, and shoulder my daypack. I cut across a stubble field and drop to all fours and crawl to the crest and peek over. I'm surprised at the smallness of the shelterbelt. The river ropes through a patchwork of willows and sloughs and mature cottonwoods, but the whole area of deer cover is only 150 yards wide in most places.

I pull up my binoculars to glass. Within seconds, a hundred yards off to my left, I find three sets of deer ears in a thicket of willows, all does. One of the deer is looking at me, the other two are unconcerned. I abruptly focus into predatorial mode. Slowly, evenly, I push my daypack in front of me and move my rifle into position. I rest my gun on the daypack for a solid rest. The crosshairs lay on the deer's neck, and the only surprise at the shot is that four deer run out of the willows instead of two.

She is a solid, handsome deer. She is bagged up, a wet doe, but by this time of year the fawns are perfectly capable of surviving on their own. I quickly slip the guts, bloodying myself barely to the wrists. I drag her to the nearest cottonwood, hang and skin her, congratulating myself on a perfect neck shot. I get the car as close as

I can, grab a game bag, and in a few more minutes I'm slamming the trunk. Driving out, the shelterbelt reminds me to check the clock. 3:48. I grin to think that I had shot, gutted, and skinned a deer in barely more time than it takes to watch a rerun of *Cheers*. I stop in Two Dot to call Kim with the story, and she's happy I'll be home early.

A few days later we butcher the deer and the next evening I pull some whitetail backstraps off the grill and say grace with my wife and three small children. The meat is tender and mild, superb eating, and we gush about the superiority of whitetails over mule deer on the table. But to me, like the rancher suggested, this venison somehow seems less sacred, more commonplace. Instead of a mystical connection to the wild and natural world, this doe is simply white packages in the freezer labeled in my wife's handwriting as "burger" or "chops". Meat. It seems too obvious to simply say it was an easy hunt.

*****

A leaden, wintry Thanksgiving afternoon, and we're all gathered, family reunion style, at Mom and Dad's. After dinner the men, militantly avoiding the board games, plop in front of the television like beached whales to cheer against the Cowboys. One of the little boys bursts in the house, leaving little boot prints of snow down the hallway behind him. He is rosy-cheeked and excited, and tells us he saw a flock of geese land on the corner of the river above the house.

Had he said "ducks" instead of "geese", nobody would have given up their warm and digestively satisfying dents on the couch. We'd all killed plenty of ducks, no big whoop in that, but a chance at a Thanksgiving goose, now that would be worth missing a few plays for. The bird hunters among us wait for a commercial and tip-toe in stocking feet across the deck and peek up the river. Sure enough. Geese.

The plan is simple and well-practiced. I'll loop upriver of the geese then walk down the bank and flush them. The geese, if they follow historical pattern, will fly down the dry channel and over the waiting guns of my brother, brother-in-law, and cousin. We bundle up the kids in their snowboots and start across the lawn. We look like a *Rugrats* movie with shotguns but, anxious and young as they are, the kids know the rule. Hunters in front, kids behind. Always. The boys start tossing snowballs at each other and we have to constantly shush them up.

*No way this is going to work. Not with all these kids. With ducks maybe, but not geese.*

At the top bend of the dry channel we line the kids up a safe distance behind the guns and the shooters take their positions. We wish each other luck, and I leave the group and pick my way through the cottonwoods to the edge of the river. A recent cold spell has the ice frozen out a couple of feet off the bank. I test it. It holds. The afternoon snow is mushy and quiet, and the gusty breeze is directly in my face. I roll my weight across my insteps as I walk, making my steps silent and smooth. I check my shotgun. It's properly loaded and my finger rests on the safety.

I stalk down the bank, stopping often, easing in against the willows as best as I can. I know I must be getting close. Out of nowhere a goose head pops up, mere feet downstream. I freeze and ready myself for the alarm honks and the rushing of wings and the failure that has so often bedeviled us with geese in the past. The river remains quiet. Seconds later, another goose head, this one preening. A goose swims out into plain view and in slam-dunk shotgun range. Another goose head, pecking at the edge of the ice. Another honker out in the water now. Spitting distance. Easy.

Why would I, a seasoned hunter, a predator, fully concentrated and fully connected, simply watch these geese, shotgun hanging uselessly from my hand? Why, when they eventually flushed, didn't my instincts react and swing the barrel with them? Why, when the expected volley of shots felled only three of the eight geese, did I tip my hat to the surviving five?

We gather back together and clean the three geese, circled by gawking kids. They want to see a goose heart. We prop open a goose and have a lesson in goose anatomy. *Here is the heart. These things that look like worms are the intestines. Here are the lungs by the backbone. This is the liver. Just like your guts, only smaller.*

I give the shooters their due about their poor shooting and, as the kids babble about the hunt, we return to our dents to cheer against the Cowboys. I keep my moment with the geese to myself, concerned about my sarcastic family and the swift verbal flogging that would surely follow any such confession. I am quietly dismayed with myself after the fact, hoping that I haven't lost my predatorial edge. My hunger. I do not want to become soft. And yet, somehow, I feel strangely liberated by the fact that for the first time in my life when the time came for the gun to go off, it had remained silent. I wondered, feared really, what it means to cross that bridge and where the road beyond might take me.

*****

About four diameters of the late September sun to go until it sets and the deer start moving. Not too much longer. I'm perched on a knob high in Wyoming's Hoback range hunting big mule deer bucks. We've been in two days and I haven't shot a buck yet, and won't unless it's a bruiser. I'd already seen about a dozen small bucks, but no shooters. I want at least a 28-incher. A 30-incher would be wonderful and to even get a shot at the monster we saw last year would be more than I could ask. I'm asking anyway. I mentally hit "rewind" and then "play" on the painfully brief video of that buck a year ago, swaggering up a scree face too steep to stand on, horns wide and golden and thick, momentarily silhouetted on the ridge as my friend Brent's gun went off. With my tag already filled that year, all I could do was watch through my binoculars as dirt spit near the bucks' hind feet at the shot. A clean miss, and in one jump the buck was into a cliffy canyon we named The Big Nasty, rugged and broken and totally unhuntable. But during the past year, when the demands of a life filled with a small business and four growing kids and increasing pressures of all kinds began to squeeze too tightly, that well-worn video was my happy place and had been more than enough motivation to get myself backpacked up here again.

A soft afternoon breeze whispers over the ridge, warm in the Indian summer weather. The Tetons loom hazily to the north, mighty and majestic, only slightly more impressive than the waves of lesser-known mountain ranges that surround me. Veins of aspens glow yellow across distant creek drainages, spectacular in contrast with the dark timber and burgundy autumn brush. It's a world-class view that prompts the feeling that indeed God is great, but even the view is less measurable than the quiet. A tenacious and permeating quiet.

A chipmunk darts up and over an old snag and then back under. It returns, flitting, pausing, flitting again. Amused, I flick a little pebble at its feet. It scurries off only to return seconds later. *A chipmunk, that's what I am.* Darting here and there and back under, trying to be everywhere at once. Although I live in a quiet little place in Montana, I do not live a quiet life in that place. Too many circumstantial and self-inflicted demands have me wound up too tight and, as if out of a slingshot, send me hurtling me across an endless flurry of busy days, weeks, years. Noisy days, start to finish. But not here. Not now. The mountain quiet is unnerving and several times during the past hour I've had a reflex to check my voice mail. Every so often I sit up and glass the basin for deer despite the warm afternoon. In between I fidget and worry, uncomfortable sitting so still for so long in so much quiet.

The mountain air is good though, and after a couple of hours of flicking pebbles at the annoyed chipmunk, I start to relax. I visualize all these hard, black globs of stress in my bloodstream, unable to survive the quiet, breaking down and dying little by little with each deep breath of purifying mountain air. When I exhale, I imagine the skeletons of these stresses drifting over the ridge on the silent breeze and vanishing across the vastness of the Hoback where they are of no consequence to anything. A flushing. A cleansing.

Just as the bottom of the sun hits the western skyline, I hear a snap in the basin below me. I catch a brownish movement disappear into the edge of the timber a half a mile away just as my binoculars focus. I glass a while without seeing anything, but I am sure I have seen something, having learned by now to trust my eyes to tell me the truth. *Probably elk, but could be a deer.* Whatever it is, I hope to get another look. I pull my gun across my lap and my daypack to my side just in case. I patiently sit and glass. Several minutes later a cinnamon colored black bear ambles out of the trees and across a little sagebrush bench. It's a big boar, probably over six feet, and he's just poking along this way and that, heading for somewhere but not in a straight line. I watch him wander with no real desire to kill him, pleasantly occupied by this bird's eye glimpse into his world, and I'm surprised that by the time he crosses back into the timber and out of sight the sun is fully set. The monster buck I'm after never appears. A couple of does pop out just before dark, but nothing else.

The mile and a half back to camp in the dark goes easily. I feel rested. Better than good. I'm mildly surprised by this, but have learned over the years that the gifts of these wild places are many and varied. I had come to Wyoming to take from the mountain a mature, full-racked muley buck, one of her greatest treasures. Instead she had taken from me a year's worth of little black knots and blown them away forever. Tonight, quite unexpectedly, I feel sanctified. My blood runs a little cleaner, my lungs a little fuller, my head a little clearer.

And, like the eating of the Alder Creek buck, I am filled.

*****

The brush to my right pops and a four point bull elk bolts up out of his bed, his head swiveled in my direction. I had no idea he was even there, but he is quartering toward me and is only about 30 yards out. I swing my bow, already drawn, away from the more distant five point, anchor and release. The bull wheels away just as the arrow is released and as he crashes through the river bottom, I can see in glimpses the fletching high and too far forward in the front shoulder. Not good. Not good at all. In three or four seconds he is out of sight and I visually mark the break in the willows where I last see him, running strong, heading for the river.

*Oh please, oh please, oh please.*

My knees aren't solid, partly because of adrenaline and partly because of the past two hours I'd spent on them sneaking on the elk. I'd already blown a chance early that morning when about 30 head beat me to a river crossing, and I chased those elk around for an hour without reward before they crossed into some posted property. I waded back to the island they originally came from to snoop around for some clues and immediately bumped a spike and a cow. I hunkered down for a while to let the elk calm down and then, on hands and knees, worked my way into the island. I found the spike, the cow, and then a five point bull. The spike, not legal to shoot, walked within twenty yards twice and finally bolted when he winded me. The cow bedded in some brush seventy yards to the west. The five point fed into a dip in the grass and never came out. I guessed he was bedded. Two hours on hands and knees to get into position for a shot, and then, just like that, a four point bull gets up and runs off with my arrow in his shoulder.

I try to calm myself. The arrow went deep, a good sign. If it went in at the right angle, it might end up in his chest cavity. If so, he's dead. If not, it would have gone into the lower neck. Not good at all. After fifteen minutes, I go to where he was standing to look for a blood trail. I find some blood twenty yards from where he was hit, but it is not good blood. Small droplets far apart. I struggle against the sinking feeling that he will not be found. Not in time anyway.

I busy myself with the blood trail. Using two arrows, one to mark last blood and one to mark new blood, I cover about 300 yards in another two and a half hours. Now it is nearly noon and seventy five degrees. Three hundred yards. I fight the urge to give up, sure now that the arrow is not in his chest. The blood peters out entirely halfway across a flat near the edge of the river. Many times I have seen elk run off this island. Always they have crossed the river into an isolated patch of brush and trees about 50 acres in size. If he is in there I can find him, but only if he lays down and bleeds. Weakens. I will return later this afternoon with some help.

I hustle my son Devin and his friend Mac to the river after football practice and set them up by the edge of the island with their bows. I want them there in case the bull spooks out of the brush and back across the river. A new hunt starts now. I take a few deep breaths, hardening my eyes, steeling myself. If he is dead, I will find him. If he is alive, there will most likely only be one chance. A flock of geese honks low overhead. I consider this to be good luck.

I wade the river and ease up the bank along the edge of the brush. So much brush to hide one elk. I pick a trail at the top of the patch and slip in. One step, maybe two. Glass. Look. Another step, maybe two. No more than two. Glass. Look. Fifteen minutes later, I ease around a willow and see an elk body big as day, a scant twenty yards ahead. I can't see the head, but I'm sure it has to be him. No unwounded elk would let me up so close so fast. I can't see any blood on the shoulder, but I draw my bow anyway and kneel, heart pumping in my ears. As I lower to my knees I see a different elk, a spike, staring right at me. He turns and trots off, and as he does the elk in front of me turns also. Another spike. I let my arrow down, cursing the spike, cursing the four point, cursing all elk.

The sun begins to set and I'm nearly through the brush patch. It's really thick near the edge of the river, and there are old elk beds everywhere. Suddenly a crashing comes about 60 yards off, and I sprint to the river as I hear the elk splash across. A small bull. I rivet my binoculars on the elk as he bolts across the flat and trots along the edge of the willows toward a hay field with his head held high. No limp. No blood. Not my bull.

I look until dark. He's not in there. I can tell my son that with confidence. Only that. I am broken otherwise.

Despite my discouragement, I sleep well. Early the next morning I leave a message at the office, and just after daybreak I'm back down on the river, looking. If the bull didn't go into the brush patch then he had to have gone farther west, downriver. I search methodically, gridding every tangle of cover back and forth, humbled and sorry. About a mile from where I shot him, I find a dollop of day-old blood on a rock at a river crossing. I gnash my teeth slightly. I am going the right direction, but the bull is not hit hard. That's for sure. He might yet die. He might fully recover. He might die slowly. These are the realities, and no matter what the circumstances of yesterday were, I have no choice but to confront the fact that my arrow, released by my own hand, is the cause of all of it. I'm being twisted down in a cold and sobering vice, only marginally comforted by the intensity of my search.

The sun grows hotter and the trail colder. I look as far as I can, finally quitting about 2:30 in the afternoon when the tank of hope finally goes empty. I work back through the brush in arcing circles, hoping for a miracle but lacking in faith. I reach the river crossing and pick up the rock with the blood. I flake some of the blood off the rock with my thumbnail and reflexively throw it in the river.

Later that day I'm at the local pole yard to pick up some fence rails. I tell Leo, a fellow hunter and a man who makes his living directly from the mountains, about my bull. He listens, and I can tell he's been there.

*He'll probably heal up fine if he went that far. Them elk are tough. If not, well, there really isn't any such thing as a wasted elk,* he tells me. *Besides, there's lots of 'em.*

I recognize the truth in what he says, although the *"besides, there's lots of 'em"* comment swallows like a hard-boiled egg going down whole. Yet, really, that is also true. Elk die every day, and the loss of one small bull to an errant arrow will have absolutely no effect on the health of the species. This I know to be true. What I also know to be true is that my lost bull is an individual member of that species, and his suffering and potential death will cast a heavy shadow on whatever joys and successes the next few days might bring, and very few failures will leave me so hollow.

*****

An hour before dawn and my pickup bounces over the cattle guard on the entrance to the freeway. I'm peering low over the steering wheel, trying to see through the growing heart shapes melting through the frost on the windshield. It is cold outside, about five degrees above. I scan the AM radio stations for something wacko to listen to until the 7 o'clock news.

Without warning, a familiar sensation warms me slightly. A hunter's vibe, an intuition, a gift of the spirit, the voice of the hunting gods speaking, *"Today is your day."* This feeling, perfectly recognizable to me over the years, occurs quite infrequently and at maddenly random intervals and yet almost always produces. I'm suddenly very confident that indeed today will be my day.

Today will also be my last day of this long and exhausting big-game hunting season. It's been great. Best ever. Back in September I killed a fantastic buck in Wyoming, not the big hog, but a great buck over 28 inches. A couple of weeks later, on a horseback hunt with my wife, I shot a decent antelope buck. I took an elk the second week of the rifle season, a small bull. My wife Kim killed a cow elk, as did Holly, my twelve year old daughter. Both Devin and Holly shot four-by-four whitetail bucks that were almost identical. Both freezers are full, and yet I felt a need to spend this final morning on the mountain in benediction to the season now past, completely ambivalent about shooting a buck. Ambivalent that is until just now, and as the heater takes the chill out of the cab and I begin to shake off the groggies, I'm surprised by the strength of the sudden desire swelling in me to fill my deer tag.

I pull off the exit, and bump up a mining road into the mountains. The hard-frozen snow groans under the tires and the sky is bitter and clear. I know where a buck is. I'd seen him with a few does in the same spot twice over the past several days. He looked to be about 24 inches, no real wall-hanger, but a decent buck with good forks and eyeguards, but I'd passed him up looking for something bigger. If he is still around this morning, I'll take him.

A few miles up the road and across from the basin where I'd seen the buck, I pull off the road and wait for light, not anxious to hike the mile in the cold unless he is up there for sure. I dig my spotting scope out of its case and attach the window mount. I roll my window halfway down, attach the scope, and look. Still too dark. Really cold air leaks into the idling truck, but I turn off the radio and breathe it in, my mind wandering.

Strange, this big-game world of mountains and hunters. I think of the mule deer buck I'm after today, that twice in the last two weeks I've had him in the crosshairs and both times let him go. I think about how full the freezers are, and if there was ever a year to simply burn a deer tag in thanksgiving, this is it. And then, just like that, the hunting gods whisper and the pilot light inside me ignites the furnace and now I really want him. I marvel about our awesome season, how blessed I am to be out hunting with my kids, how thankful for the times with my wife and the many precious hours outside alone, and I actually start to sadden about next year, previous experience with the laws of averages suggesting leaner times ahead. Like much of life, this passion for hunting is ripe with paradox. I want the deer I don't want. I'm sad about our wonderful year.

Daylight comes and the buck shows up with his does. I turn the truck off and gear up. Looking over the situation, I need to circle to the south to keep the wind in my favor and hike up the second wash from the creek bottom for cover. I glass the hillside where the deer are grazing. Other than a sprinkling of juniper trees, the basin is open and huntable. Should be a piece of cake.

Forty minutes later I'm crawled against the base of a scrubby cedar tree, resting my rifle over a branch, waiting for a couple of does to move from in front of the buck seventy five yards away. I breathe out of my mouth downward to avoid fogging the scope and watch the buck. He is swollen-necked and bossy, full of rut. He sticks his nose out and curls his upper lip, the estrus of a doe charging his entire self, filling the measure of his creation. Yet I know that it is not this rutty buck but the does that are the keepers of the species, and when this buck is removed from the herd another will be in his place by morning.

Moments later the buck chases a doe out to the edge of the herd and turns broadside. I shoot. The buck kicks with both hind legs and then just stands there, the does bounding away in all directions like popcorn popping. I chamber another shell but know it won't be necessary. Seconds later he is down.

It's too cold to lolly-gag much, but I take a moment and give thanks.

*I knew it!*

I gut and tag him, not at all surprised how deeply the scent of mule deer buck on a cold morning continues to affect me. I tie my drag strap to his antlers and halter hitch his nose, and he slides nicely over the sugary snow. I break a good sweat dragging him, but I'm happy I'm here, by myself with this buck on this cold, November mountain. It's the right day for this and I feel good. Refreshed. Reinvigorated. A crisp morning, a nice buck, a clean kill. Since the freezers are full and I refuse to waste any meat, I determine to make jerky out of this buck and give it to the primary children at church, sharing with them in some small way a piece of this morning, this place, this buck.

I pause with my deer and look into his lifeless blue eyes. Moral logic might say I did wrong this morning, to shoot a buck that I really didn't need. I wholeheartedly agree with moral logic and yet, at this moment, I remain pleased and unremorseful. Unconflicted. I stand and absorb the panorama of Rocky Mountains that surround me, frozen and snowbound, illuminated by the brittle aqua sky. A cold haze blankets the valleys in frost, the visible world a startling contrast of sky blue and forest green and pure white. It comes to me that the right or wrong of pulling the trigger this morning cannot be judged on an equation of linear logic. There is a spiritual fiber in the cloth of nature, a non-logic, a reckless chaos that somehow produces harmony and symmetry. A time to kill and a time to heal, a time to act and a time to be acted upon, the one or the other or both at the same time.

This thought balances well, feels right. I think of the seeds of spring buried under the snows of the frozen peaks, grasses and berries and purple wildflowers. I think of the mule deer fawns fathered by the buck at my feet, curled up under those grasses, spotted and still. More truth seems close now, the frigid mountain morning seemingly willing to part the curtains for a glimpse into the Grand Scheme and the Almighty Power of God that directs it. The truth that swirls around the reality of every organism on this indescribable planet, all blended together in violence and tranquility. Systems atomic- so small that no one has ever seen, to systems cosmic- so immense that no one can comprehend, complex beyond comprehension, each a synergistic part of the whole yet existing in its own sphere and element. I settle for a moment on the thought of the planet earth and the extreme improbability of her perfectly placed and methodical rotations around the sun, not too far and not too close. I think again of the miraculous cycle of snowpack on those frozen peaks, piling up all winter to bleed out all summer, literally providing life for the creeks and rivers and valleys below. I consider the migrations of steelhead and snow geese, the hibernation of bears and fruit trees, the limitless potential of life in a bucket of dirt.

And for a moment I consider myself and my place in this grand and glorious Creation. Without warning an internal feeling of wellness surges in me, an awakening, with a certainty that me and this dead buck and this frozen piece of earth all somehow deeply matter, despite our microscopic stature in the universe and the absolute assurance that we are all dust to dust. The fleeting vision fades. I grasp for it, for more meaning and understanding, but I can only hold the very fringe of it, and then it is gone.

But even this is enough. I am filled.

## OPEN AND SHUT

*"All flesh shall perish together, and man shall turn again unto*
*dust.*
*If now thou hast understanding, hear this" Job 34:15-16*

I knew from the instant I set the hook that this was a big, solid fish. He picked up the lure about two-thirds through the run and, once hooked, ripped upstream and held in the deepest part of the hole. I wound down on him, keeping the line tight, and popped him with another hook set. Needing better leverage, I waded upstream under the willows until I was sideways of him. He augured into the bottom of the hole and refused to budge. For about fifteen minutes we battled tug-of-war. The rod bent double right out of the cork, but my drag was good and my line was fresh. I had a decent chance of seeing this fish. For a long time the only movement in the pole was a gentle up-and-down swaying at the tip, keeping cadence with the big fish's tail wafting back and forth in the current.

Gradually I was able to work him in toward me but once he hit the edge of the blue water he quickly took back the fifteen yards of line I had gained. Gradually he drifted in, quickly back out. Gradually in, quickly out. Five or six times. I thought he was beginning to tire, so the next time he worked in I thumbed down on the spool of my reel for more tension and pulled him out of the blue water and into the shallows. He came up readily enough and for a second I could see the chartreuse lure firmly in the corner of his mouth. Then his belly must have hit bottom.

The fish exploded upstream, peeling line off the reel so fast that it took the first layer of skin off my thumb. Three or four times he jumped wildly, splashing back in with an awkward splunk. All I could do was beller out a war-whoop and hang on and keep my thumb off the reel. Oh Yeah! This was the mighty king salmon. This was wild Alaska. This was tundra and grizzlies and darkless summer nights. This was float-planes and rafts and hacking a campsite out of the bush with oars. And this was going to be over fast if the fish got out of the smooth water.

I nervously eyed the amount of line left on my reel when the big salmon suddenly reversed course and streaked straight down river. Blurting out a bad word, I cranked madly on the reel trying to keep the slack out of the line as he ran toward me and then past me. This was very bad news. The day before, I watched as a fish I was fighting cleared the pool and shot downstream into the rapids. Every inch of line had quickly unspooled off my singing reel as if I had casted into traffic and hooked the bumper of a bus. Kersnap! All I could do was reel up my fishless line and tip my hat. But this fish turned and skimmed the riffle at the tail out and circled back into the smooth water, and after two more spectacular jumps, he bored again into the deepest part of the hole.      Twenty minutes later he lay subdued in the little side channel we were using as a landing. His shoulders were as thick as a pig's and he weighed about the same as a Costco-sized bag of dog food. Measuring him with my rod he went 52 inches, which is huge for this river system. He was crimson red with prehistoric teeth and a nasty hooked jaw. I gently hefted him for a few photos and released him.

I was tired and jazzed and thirsty. What an awesome fish! I leaned my rod against the willows and sat down on the river bank, digging a juice out of my gear bag. I couldn't get the image of that huge fish, subdued on his side, the white of his belly rocking gently with the little waves in the landing channel, his mouth gaping open and shut and open and shut. His brassy eyes looked me right in the face. He was surely dying right then, but he seemed willing enough. There was no fear or pain in those unblinking eyes. Or shame. He seemed at once defiant and resigned. Defiant over what for him must have been a very bizarre experience and yet resigned to accept the outcome which would have been two or three sharp cracks to the head with a fish whomper except for the fillets of a different salmon already in the cooler. But he did not die that day. After the photos, I righted him into the current of the landing, needing both hands to hold the base of his tail, and moved him back and forth into the current. When enough oxygenated water had passed through him to restore his senses he motorboated out of the channel and back into the deep blue water. Defiance. Resignation. Fear. Shame. Certainly I give too much to a fish.

But there was, for me at least, some undeniable quality in the moment when that mighty fish lay dying on his side with his jaws gaping open and shut and me looking into his unflinching eyes. It was futile to release him, and I did not set him free out of any notion of political correctness or sportsmanship. He was going to die soon anyway. Within three months that great fish and every single one of its kind, literally millions and millions of fish, would be dead. Every single one. No survivors. Nature has genetically imposed upon the king salmon, as all species of salmon, to die shortly after spawning. These kings were migrating up the river to spawn. Consequently, my fish and every one like him would again that summer lay dying on their sides, spilling what life was left in their soft and wasted bodies into the river, their brassy eyes unblinking, their mouths gaping open and shut and open and shut and finally just open.

The enormity of this circle of death is most tangible on the water. When I wasn't at the oars of the raft, I'd often lie over the tubes and look into the river with my polarized sunglasses. I saw kings in the pools behind rocks, in the deeper runs, strung out single-file in the riffles, seemingly everywhere. Schools of two or ten or fifty, all running upstream. To our sanitized minds, the thought that every single one of them would soon be dead is simply catastrophic. Like we should DO something. Like we should increase funding or raise awareness or have a rally or a "Save the Salmon" concert or something.

We floated into a spot one afternoon where a little creek swirled into the river. The bottom of the river was painted red with the salmon stacked up there. We pulled over at that spot and fished for two days. It was phenomenal fishing, every red smear in the current beguiling us into casting over and over. We could reach the fish here with our flyrods. I can tell you that no matter what experience you have in fly-fishing, wherever you have been in the world, whatever species you have caught, that you will never forget the explosiveness of a forty-five pound king salmon on a nine-weight. After two days of witnessing the masses of salmon coming up the river we knew we were only touching a sacramental percentage of the fish. And soon they would all be dead.

I was poking around one afternoon at this place, looking for a few new fish to cast to, when I crossed a shallow gravel bar at the edge of the river. Dozens of little seashells in the shape of miniature thread spools littered the gravel wash. I picked one up, but it wasn't a seashell at all. It was a section of vertebrae from the spine of a long-dead king salmon. I gathered a few in my palm. Some were plainly fresher than others, a grim testament to the fish's will to sustain the species, and I wondered if the salmon whose bones I held in my hand was a great-grandparent or great-great-grandparent to the fish we ate for dinner last night. I thought of my fish, how his vertebrae might one day litter this spot, and how it was possible that I might once more hold him in my hands should I ever come back.

Finishing my juice, I lay back against the willows, swatting aimlessly at mosquitoes. In the hazy distance, Mt. McKinley loomed absurdly large in the cloudless sky, a rare treat. I knew that no photograph could begin to do justice to the largesse of the morning, but I took a few anyway. This was my fourth trip down the river and I had previously caught dozens of kings, yet none had pierced me like this last one and I wasn't sure why.  Later I wondered if maybe the brassy eyes of that great fish struck me because of my age. At almost 40, I'm beginning to sense the possibility that, like the fish, my own life might be short lived. Of course I've always known that none of us are getting out of here alive. I've always known it but now I'm old enough to start to believe it. Recently, I went so far as to hire a lawyer and write out a will, going directly against a deeply embedded superstition that making out a will is somehow the same as making out a permission slip to die. And I do not want to die. Maybe I was actually terrified by the image of my salmon subdued in the shallows. Terrified because one day at the scene of a car wreck or at a cancer clinic or in a nursing home I will unavoidably be just like he was, helplessly dying on my side, gaping for breath, eyes glassy. Or even more terrifying, that these things might happen prematurely to someone I love. These are, of course, horrible thoughts and I have, to one degree or other, learned to deal with them with the exact qualities I mistakenly gave to my fish. Defiance. Resignation. Fear. Shame. But mostly I have learned fear, and when such thoughts of mortality appear I usually hit the remote and simply change the channel. But sometimes the channel won't change.

I was thirteen carefree years old the day my parents huddled myself and my siblings around the sofa on the greenish shag carpet and Mom sobbed out the news that Uncle Blayne had leukemia and that it was quite advanced. I had absolutely no idea what leukemia was, but I knew it must be very bad. My father, his voice breaking, lead us in a prayer invoking the Almighty to spare Uncle Blayne. *Spare Uncle Blayne?* The words hit my young spine like ice water.

"Could Uncle Blayne die from leukemia?" I asked.

"Oh, yes, but with God all things are possible and perhaps He will cure him. But it doesn't look good, either. It will take a miracle."

Without my permission, great tears suddenly welled up in my eyes and a tight lump formed in my throat. Quickly I turned away. I was ashamed of those tears and those that would follow. Uncle Blayne? Dead? My Uncle Blayne, the one who could always strike us out at whiffleball with that nasty curveball? Uncle Blayne, who always had a story about fly fishing or deer hunting or baseball? My five cousins - the youngest a mere toddler - their Dad dead? With tears still flowing I resolved to face this like a man, unafraid and with courage. And when I was unable to do so, whenever the knot in my throat formed or the tears seeped up, I turned away and taught myself how not to think about it.

One day, very near the end, my Mom and Dad returned from a weekend of helping my Aunt Carla and being with Uncle Blayne. As a matter of courtesy, not really wanting to know, I asked my Dad how he was doing.

"He is very sick and very weak. But," Dad said, "he is looking forward to the experience."

It's funny in life how often innocent little sentences scratch way deeper than intended and leave a lasting mark. Looking forward to the experience? Looking forward to dying like I was looking forward to Christmas and getting my drivers license? The idea of it completely horrified me. So far, every thought of Uncle Blayne's death had petrified me into a tearless stupor and yet at that moment I thought of him, bald from the chemo and shivering with stomach cramps in a hospital bed. I imagined Uncle Blayne staring down the Grim Reaper with his quirky little smile and offering to shake his hand. Could he actually look forward to stepping into the big dark? If it were truly so, if it was even possible, then that would change everything.

My teenage guts froze solid before the dreaded family viewing. I had seen dead people at funerals before, but they had been old and I hadn't known them well and I had been told that it was a blessing. This was different. This was tragedy. When I finally made my way to the casket, he was in there all right. It looked just like him, only a little waxy or something, and I thought that he had done it. He had had the experience. He had looked forward to it and he had done it. Ready or not. Afraid or not. At the funeral when the tears came I just let them go, and I wondered in a place deep inside me if life would ever find me in such pain or sick enough or man enough to actually look forward to the experience. Maybe the brassy eyes of my king salmon found my secret, in telling me that he was ready and reminding me that I was not.


I'm at the oars on a postcard-perfect summer afternoon a few days later and near the end of our 70 mile float. The river is quieter here, so I lean back against the gear net and watch Alaska drift by. Huge cottonwoods overhang the river and filter the dizzying sky. Great pods of ferns drape the bank and seagulls hang lazily in the air and squawk on the gravel bars. As we bobble along, a mother merganser and about a dozen fuzzy little baby mergansers skitter across the river and under a cut bank on the other side. A grayling surfaces. Little hatches of mayflies dap up and down on the mirrored surface of the water. Every living organism existing in its own sphere and element, apparently finding joy in the measure of their creation. I think of my fish, hatched among the pea gravel of the spawning redds and nourished by the yolk sack it was provided with by its long-dead mother. Then, ironically, he continued to be nourished by the broken down proteins from the carcasses of the thousands of parent salmon washing down the river. He continued to grow and then, for a reason nobody can explain, he and all his generation of smolt king salmon turned downstream and migrated down the river systems to the sea. Guessing from his size and weight, he probably spent about five or six years in the ocean. No one knows for sure where he went and what he did out there in the ocean, but he must have been eating well. Early this spring, having survived the overwhelming list of dangers that by now had claimed over ninety percent of his siblings, he and his generation gathered at the mouth of the Big Suisitna and started upstream. On July 5, I caught him at a place we call Sunflower Creek, three major river forks from the ocean and more than likely the exact place he was born.

Such complexity in life and such certainty of death. Such mystery and such paradox. But it is too much to think about today. Much too much. I am too tired and with so little time left in Alaska,

I dismiss the thoughts and simply raft and let the air in and the defenses down. Only a few hours more and we'll load the float-plane and head home. It would be best to try and unwind as many knots as possible. The time goes by quickly.


Bleary and sleep deprived from too much fishing and the red-eye flight from Anchorage, I gather my stuff and sprawl on a lounge chair in the Seattle airport. It's just after 5:00 A.M, and I have about a 3 hour layover until my connecting flight home. The place is pretty empty except for the occasional snack vendor and airline worker. I doze off. When I wake up, the place is packed and moving. Streams of people are pushing up the concourses. They funnel off the main concourse and split here or there heading for this wing or that. Once they hit their gates, they all pool up and crowd the waiting areas and phone banks.

Lifting out of my sleepy fog, still clutching my rod case, it occurs to me that these people are just like the salmon. But instead of Sunflower Creek or Lower Yenlo they are schooled up and headed for Gate D-4 or C-11 and whatever destinies lie beyond. Because it's been on my mind, I also think that every one of them, just like the salmon, must eventually die.

That guy over there on the cell phone? He's toast. The pretty lady with the drag along suitcase? A goner. That fat guy ordering a McMuffin? Sooner than later it looks like. The old lady on the electric cart? She may never see snow again. The little kid with the teddy-bear backpack? Hate to think about it. The couple over there hugging good-bye? Their bones will probably rot away side-by-side in some manicured cemetery. The cocky pilot whooshing by? He might have cancer right now and not even know it and be dead in six months. For that matter, I might have cancer right now and be dead in six months.

And right then, in the Seattle airport of all places, still drunk on Alaska, I was not afraid. For just a flicker I was looking forward to the experience.

**A HOME OF OUR OWN**

*"And that which fell among thorns are they, which,
when they have heard, go forth, and are choked
with cares and riches and pleasures of this life,
and bring no fruit to perfection." Luke 8:14*

Our first home together cost only $150.00 a month, a frugal but hard-fought rent that I had personally negotiated with the landlord. Even for Rexburg, Idaho in 1985, it was a real bargain. It wasn't until after the honeymoon, when I swept up my brand new bride for the traditional threshold crossing, that I first got an inkling that maybe it wasn't such a good deal after all. With her arms locked around my neck, about to see for the first time the start of our new life together, Kim looked seductively into my eyes. After a week of honeymooning, I knew exactly where that look was heading. Grinning, I reached under her knees, twisted the doorknob, and pushed the door open.

Her eyes left mine and she looked around the apartment and then flashed back to my face, gut-shot.

"You're kidding, right?"

"Nope," I said. "Can you believe it? One hundred and fifty a month!"

She absolutely could not believe it. The two-inch turquoise shag carpet, the green vinyl sofa with the back legs broken off, the fresh paint over the mold in the shower, the super-single rubber mattress waterbed. But it was true, only $150.00 a month, and it was all ours for at least the next five months.

I asked her to be patient. We had big plans, the two of us. A beautiful house in the country, a few horses grazing in the pasture, a few kids playing on the trampoline. A home of our own nestled somewhere in the shadows of the Rocky Mountains. But right then we were just a couple of newly-wed college kids, scraping hard just to meet the $150.00 rent, light years from wherever that place might really be. Neither of us had trust funds or rich families or wealthy relatives about to die. We would have to earn those dreams from scratch. Later that night I told Kim about a wise saying I heard that went, "I'll live like you won't and then I'll live like you can't."

"Well, you certainly got a good start on the first part," she said.

A few days later some guys moved into the upstairs apartment. Nearly every weekend they'd start the party about midnight and carry on until way past the wee hours, the loud bass of the music thumping relentlessly through the thin walls. We were both working odd hours and the lack of sleep and the incessant WHUMP, WHUMP, WHUMP of the music started to fray our nerves. We would lay awake on those sleepless nights, stacked on each other on the super single waterbed, talking of our future and our options for shutting the party down. Once I thumped on the ceiling with a broomstick, reminding them we were still awake down here at 2:47 AM. The music went from WHUMP, WHUMP, WHUMP, to whump, whump, whump, but then you could hear the chatter and bursts of laughter and feet shuffling. We lay in bed, staring at the ceiling, making up the place where we would live in our own quiet house in the country, far away from unwanted parties and turquoise shag carpet and moldy bathrooms.

One day I needed to shut the power off to fix something in our apartment. The landlord told me where the breaker box was and I found, with tremendous delight, that the main electrical breakers for each of the four apartments were on a telephone pole behind the building in a choke of weeds. The next weekend, I let the party go until about 2 o'clock and then I went out and threw the breaker marked "# 4" . The lights in the upstairs corner windows went pitch black and the music went WHUMP, WHU...... There was a long silence. I crouched low in the weeds.

"Duude, the power went out," somebody finally said.

A few minutes later a couple of cars started and the party drove away. I snuck back into our apartment. We laughed until the tears flowed.

"Duude," I mocked. "The power went out!"

At 6:30 on my way to work, I walked out to the pole and threw the breaker back on. WHUMP, WHUMP, WHUMP. With great pleasure I heard the sleepy moan and the stumble across the floor and the music screech off. I had to throw that breaker three or four more times before we moved. They never did figure it out.


Our second home was free, and it wasn't long before we found out that that wasn't a bargain either. Morehead State in Kentucky had recruited me to play football but didn't have much experience with married players and didn't quite know how to meet the obligation of the scholarship to provide housing for the both of us. They finally put us in Married Student Housing, which amounted to a few acres of very old and very small blue trailer homes without air conditioning that also had an unreal ability to conduct heat.

Back then everything we owned fit into the bed of our Toyota pickup, and with a great sense of adventure we unpacked our stuff into our blue trailer. Thirty minutes later Kim put out the finishing touch, a set of red 12-inch candles and brass candle holders we got as a wedding gift.

The late August weather was unbearable. The arid heat of Idaho was no match for the insta-sweat combination of heat and humidity in eastern Kentucky. Our house was the little blue trailer that could, and it soaked up the heat like an ant soaks up the beam from a magnifying glass. A few days later, Kim picked me up from a football practice late in the afternoon and drove us home. The air inside was like a blast furnace.

"Oh, no," Kim said. I looked over, and I swear this is true, the 12-inch candles were drooped over the candle holders from the heat. Besides that, the school was uninspiring and we were 1 and 10 for the year in football. Kim made a bunch of music-box teddy bears that I sold door-to-door at Christmas for the money we needed to move back West. We couldn't get back to the Rocky Mountains soon enough.

We transferred to Brigham Young University, and our next apartment was so small that our pickup load of stuff actually made it look full. We slept on a queen-sized mattress tossed right on the floor, having abandoned the newly-married utility of the super-single. Our first child Devin was born to us here. We had him at a birthing center that had a "short-stay" and a "long-stay" option. The short-stay option, which unbelievably we chose, was discharge from the clinic six hours after birth. So there I was in our apartment, a mere six hours after his birth, holding this tiny little body that I had absolutely no idea what to do with. And there was Kim, lying on a mattress on the floor, overcome from her first experience with childbirth, the brutality of which neither of us was really prepared for.

And, like the Grinch Who Stole Christmas, my heart grew three sizes that day. My beautiful wife would not have to lay on a mattress on the floor her whole life. I would get her a real bed in a real house for crying out loud. My little boy would learn from me to hunt and to fish and to work and to be a good person and to play the game of football. I would graduate from college, take that education into the lone and dreary world, and make our lives come true. My family would have it, that house in the country. I would see to it. It was still light years away, but that tiny little body wriggling in my awkward arms and the picture of Kim sleeping on the floor gave me a tremendous, if not suffocating, resolve.

A few apartments later, and a year or so after graduation, we bought our first house in Menan, Idaho. It was a miniature cinder-block house we bought on a contract-for-deed from Grandpa Beyeler for $24,000.00 and no money down. Years later I bought a new pickup from my lifelong friend Scott who is in the car business and complained to him about the price.

"This truck is more than my first house," I said.

"This truck is nicer than your first house," he countered.

There wasn't much I could say to that.

But before we moved, we used a power company incentive to insulate the house and put up some siding. We made a thousand dollars when we sold. Our home in the country suddenly seemed only as far away as the moon.

We bounced around between jobs, finding our way, and had another baby, a girl we named Holly. In 1989, I accepted a job selling paper and industrial products up in Montana with Dixon Paper Company, a privately held company based out of Denver. We looked all over for a home in the country, but ended up with a house right in the middle of Helena that we got in a sealed-bid auction. It was a HUD repo and it was cheap. We painted it, fixed the fences and decks, sheet-rocked the garage, and had two more kids, Jacob and Jessi. That gave us two boys and two girls.

The first three years in this house were, at least from a career perspective, quite rewarding and profitable. This job provided us, for the first time in our married lives, with a few extra dollars at the end of the month. We saved that money and started looking at land, and Kim crowded the night-stand with house plan magazines. By now the Big Sky of Montana fit us like a pair of comfortable boots, and it seemed that our home in the country was at least in the atmosphere. I hoped so anyway. I secretly began to worry that the pace I was working was unsustainable. Then, without warning, the company I worked for was sold to International Paper, one of the largest paper-related companies in the world. We were told not to worry, that it would be a "seamless transition". It was, in fact, just exactly that. The seams came completely apart and policy change after hostile policy change eventually left me with very little emotional reserve, not to mention greatly reduced financial potential. When I first approached the possibility of a change, Kim would hear nothing of it, fearing that the home she could just about see in the fringes of our future would be rudely yanked away. But one day a few months later, after a meeting with my manager to resolve some grievances had ended poorly, she squarely and bluntly told me to do what I had to do.

Above our bed, in the plaster pattern on the ceiling, was the vague outline of an old Indian chief. That Indian friend of mine and I got to know each other very well over the next few months. I spent hundreds of sleepless hours staring at him in the dim, street-lit dark of night planning my big jump. We went over the math of the "best-case scenario" and "worst-case scenario" umpteen hundred times. I fretted endlessly over cash-flow and bankers and fear. Well before I felt I was ready, the Great Chief whispered that it was now or never.


The next day I walked my resignation letter to the big blue mailbox on the corner, a block from the house. I held it in the jaws of that mailbox for a long time. That home of our own out in the country, the horses, the trampoline, all of it, felt mighty slippery right then. Before, when I had quit the insurance business or selling cars, I had nowhere to go but up the economic ladder. This time I had something to lose. A lot to lose, and I knew perfectly well and with a great sense of foreboding that it was possible that I might be pushing our house in the country ten or twelve or thirty calendars in the future. I finally let the letter go. We were now self-employed distributors of packaging and shipping supplies. It took three or four miles of walking before I ended up back at the house.

One more fixer-upper, a land sale, and after seven focused and determined years of work, we moved into our brand new house around Groundhog's Day of the year 2,000. We had been fifteen years of scrapping and saving, buying and selling, painting and fixing. From out of somewhere light years away, our dream now has a front porch, a two car garage, and a refrigerator that makes its own ice. We earned it from scratch, Kim and I. The house is beautiful, spacious, and functional. Adequate in every way. It sits on 55 acres of ground, on an agricultural bench near the tiny town of Drummond in western Montana. There are a few horses grazing in the pasture and the kids chatter carelessly on the trampoline and no matter which direction you look a mountain range looks back. By the grace of God, and after fifteen years of incredible effort, we finally get to sleep in our dream.

For fifteen years I had looked forward to a well-deserved rest once we finally moved into our new house. During that time, especially when I was really tired and still had a hundred miles until home, I visualized allowing myself to slow down once the house was finally built. My plan was to move in, take a little break, and then Kim and I would saddle up and ride off into the sunset to live happily ever after.

On a bitter November morning, nine months after we moved into the house, I'm outside scraping the frost off the windshield of my truck to go to work. It's past 9:30, plenty late to be getting started. I hadn't been working out or reading the paper or doing paperwork. I hadn't done anything, really. No spark. No zest. No energy. A few weeks before I had to buy new pants, size forty, and go through the closet and toss out the thirty-eights. Normally a religious exerciser, I can't honestly remember the last week when I worked out more than twice. And now I need new pants. I just can't seem to stay motivated. Or focused.

I bump down the frozen gravel road and look south to the snow-dusted mountains of Upper Willow Creek. Maybe what I need is to get packed up and go on a big-time three-day elk hunt this weekend. Like I used to. Yes, that would help. The thought stirs me slightly, but I decide it's just too much trouble to go to right now. It would be easier to hunt someplace close for a morning or two. For me, it's an unbelievable, piercing thought. It should have been the final straw, the dagger through the soul, and yet I don't even blink. That particular thought is no more unexpected or inexplicable or incomprehensible than any of the many others of the last few months.

I'd honestly tried to take a break after the exhausting chaos of moving in, but instead of getting refreshed, I became even more tired. The more I slept in, the worse I felt. The worse I felt, the less I did. The less I did, the worse I slept. The worse I slept, the more I slept in. And, of course, the more I slept in, the worse I felt again. The ebb and flow of this cycle tormented me for months. I was caught totally flat-footed by this powerful, aimless melancholy. I was unaware that there would be, or could be, anything other than bliss and satisfaction after the hard work of realizing your goal. Nobody had warned me otherwise, that there might be evil snakes in the grass even after your dream comes true. Perhaps especially after the dream comes true, the strange, paradoxical consequences like the profound feelings of emptiness exactly at the moment when I should be the most satisfied.

The fog that swirled over me completely bypassed Kim. She was as happy as a puppy with two peters, decorating her new house and singing along to her Garth Brooks music. Sometimes her happiness was infectious, other times it was annoying. She could plainly see I was struggling, but she didn't know how to help me. Well, I didn't know how to help me either.

Looking back, I guess I still got out and did a few things and managed to keep the business going and, for that matter, kept up a pretty good face. It wasn't like I was institutional or popping Prozac or anything like that. But undeniably, like our candles in the blue trailer, the candle that normally flickered bright and vigorous inside me had drooped over the candlestick. Eventually I swam out of it, except for those pesky ten pounds, after it finally dawned on me that the reason I was drowning wasn't because I couldn't swim, but because I didn't have a finish line. I also found out that it's really hard to slow down after so many years in overdrive. It's like trying to drive 55 across Nevada. A full year passed before I began to accept the slower pace of the white lines. I had to force myself to pull over once in a while to see a sunset or a baby horse. I had to teach myself again how to stand still and take a deep breath and listen to the wind. I had to lace up my exercise shoes. I had to make myself get up and go hunting. I had to remind myself constantly that no matter what I was seeing to look for the beauty. And, after a long hiatus, I had to once again pause long enough to find meaning in the world and then write it down.

Not long ago a friend asked me what we would change about the house now that we have lived in it a while. I told him that when you have lived in some of the places we have lived and then get to live in a house like this, well, you feel pretty blessed and I wouldn't change a thing. And that is truly how it is. I wouldn't change a single thing. Not now. I told my friend that I had learned a lot along the way, most recently how wonderful it was to remember how good ice-cold milk tastes right out of the jug. He smiled weakly, completely oblivious.

Occasionally, the mysterious funk still plagues me, but I'm on to it now and not so baffled by it. I have come to understand that the root of my depression had two stems. I think, in part, that the frenetic and self-imposed pace of the journey simply overwhelmed me. That, and I suppose I was the greyhound that ran and ran, as fast as he could, and finally caught the tin rabbit.

# RHYTHMS

*"…neither are your ways my ways, saith the Lord.*
*For as the heavens are higher than the earth,*
*so are my ways higher than your ways"*
*Isaiah 55:8-9*

I studied the hoof prints mashed into the snow on the logging road. A big elk, and all by itself. The fronts of the toes splayed wide. Distinct dew claws. The tops of the hooves dragging lazily over the snow. Almost certainly a bull. Even better, these tracks were smoking fresh. I happened to be out moose hunting, a rare treat in Montana due to the lottery odds of drawing a tag, and I'd wandered up this unfamiliar logging road on a tip from a local guy in the restaurant who said he had seen a giant bull moose up here a couple of days ago. Even though I'd set my precious moose tag prominently over the elk tag in my wallet, I wasted little time on my decision. I'd killed an elk for seven years in a row and really wanted to keep the streak going. Besides, I had almost three weeks left on the moose hunt but my elk season would close with the setting of the sun two hours away.

The wind drifted in breezes into my face and the chinook air had the afternoon snow mushy and quiet. The elk tracks roped out of a chute of steep timber, crossed the logging road, and meandered into a broad bench of lodgepole which quite conveniently situated itself about a mile above a Forest Service road. Perfect. I knew full well the opportunity that I'd stumbled into, a gift really, and I knelt for a moment and asked the Almighty for guidance and success. Taking my meat from the mountains is serious business for me, religious even, and I took the time to shut my eyes into the wind and channel my energies with a few deep breaths. When I felt ready, I downshifted into hunting speed and steeled my eyes.

The snow held better in the timber, and I knelt to feel the edges of a track. Even bigger that I thought. I stamped my foot next to the track and the snow showed no difference. Fresh indeed. No doubt this elk carried antlers, probably big antlers. Maybe even huge. I thought of pulling into the driveway with a giant six-point bull that I'd tracked down in the timber on the last day of the season. I am somewhat famous for being able to catch a fish on my last cast, and I felt sure that karma would smile on me today. Even so, there could be no mistakes. I'd have to hunt well, but I somehow felt that these tracks would lead to a freezer full of elk meat. Unslinging the rifle off my shoulder, I checked the chamber and the safety and started tracking.

It didn't take long for the elk to show why he was still alive. He stuck to the timber, always skirting the open meadows. His tracks would wander through the trees for a couple hundred yards and then he'd gain a little elevation and fish hook back, then continue on in the direction he was going. I considered this to be coincidence the first couple of times, after that I wasn't so sure. Several times I saw where he'd nibbled at the brownish leaves of a willowy shrub, and I knelt down and inspected the track again to make sure this wasn't an immature moose. No, these tracks belonged to an elk. When I stood up, force of habit caused me to sling my rifle over my shoulder. Grimacing, I caught myself and braced it back at arms. There would most likely be one, quick chance. I had to be ready.

The bull had moved along unhurried and deliberate. I did the same. After a while I came to a smattering of tracks and in the center of them was a pee hole the size of a quarter. Maybe for good luck, maybe for a connection, maybe for no good reason at all, I made a pee hole right next to his. After that the tracks bobbed and weaved all over the place. I slowed again. I prayed again. I steeled myself again. The bull was getting ready to bed down.

About a hundred yards later I found his bed, but he was gone. To my anguished relief, he hadn't been spooked. He had fed across a little hillside, once again staying in the timber between a couple of small meadows. Ahead of me the tracks pugged over a little ridge, and something powerful inside told me he was right there, just over that ridge. I positively knew it. The breeze wafted perfect into my face. I thought I could smell him. He was there all right. I lifted my nose into the breeze, and in my mind I saw him, blonde and big with long chocolate horns, polished points bobbing as he nibbled unaware on those little leaves. I saw myself crawl over the ridge and find him in the scope and shoot him in the lungs. I even saw him in the back of my truck, while I backed up to the shop as the kids bounded out of the house and Kim said, "Wow, that's a big one!"

I shook the thoughts from my head. I couldn't get distracted like that. Minutes later, and on my hands and knees, I eased over the little ridge and scanned the draw with my binoculars. More tracks. More timber. No elk.

I stood and brushed the snow off my pants, cradling my rifle. He had been here. It should have happened right here. I had no choice but to keep on, even though the tracks had somehow lost their strength. The elk was feeding more now, the snow swirled around stubs of grass in plate-sized circles, and I would have bet my house that he was in rifle range at that exact moment. If only I could freeze time, lift the timber out of the way for ten seconds, and lay it down again. I stood quiet for a minute, listening. Feeling. For the first time I noticed the darkness closing in. My last cast.

Ten minutes later it was over. Hunkered on his tracks, I sensed a flash a hundred yards to my left through the timber. Almost faster than I could see. A single frame in the movie. Over. Done. I followed the tracks to his bed just in case. Big, double gouges of snow sprayed out of the tracks racing through the trees, and I followed until they finally left the timbered ridge and the tracks pocked downhill across a giant clear-cut, the hoof prints four feet apart. I imagined him again, stepping out like a gaited horse, nose high, antlers laid back to his flanks, ears pinned back, crossing the clear-cut and disappearing into the dark timber beyond.

From the upper edge of the ridge I hopelessly glassed away the last five minutes of daylight, completely hollow and betrayed. Hadn't I prayed sincerely? Hadn't I hunted well? And yet I was left with nothing more than the teasing tracks of a spooked elk splattered across this clear-cut, mocking my failure. Why not bless me on this final day? Why even show me the track? A movement below me at the edge of the opening jolted me out of my pathos. Reflexively, hopefully, my binoculars focused on the spot.

Hunters. Two of them, and they walked oblivious below me right across the middle of the clear-cut on a logging road. I could hear their voices chattering, laughter sprinkling in the cooling air. When they hit the bull's tracks they stopped and looked, but no longer than a few seconds, and then kept walking away, rifles slung over their shoulders.

For some reason a bitterness swelled in me, and I was suddenly angry that they had even become a part of it.

*****

We made the intersection at Grassrange just before midnight and pulled over to de-caffeinate. I stepped out of the truck and a gust of wind nearly ripped the door from my hand. The temperature and the wind were both in the forties, and I silently swallowed the thought that I knew this trip was going to be a bad idea. We wisely kept our backs to the wind, sprinkling the road in front of us, and when we got back in the truck John reminded me to slow down for fear of deer on the road. John had driven the first three hours to Great Falls, where we stopped to fuel up and change drivers. Since then we had mostly talked about religion, which would have been unusual on a hunting trip except that it was Sunday and John, suffering some bootprint-in-the-face consequences for a few bad decisions, had just recently put Jesus back in his life.

I really hadn't wanted to suffer the eight hour drive to Jordan, Montana just for an antelope, already exhausted from an October crammed full with an Idaho elk hunt, an Idaho mule deer hunt, three weeks of coaching junior high football, work, and four

7

weekends of watching my kids play football and volleyball. But the circumstances with John softened me, so I hastily gathered up my gear and my antelope tag, kissed Kim good-bye, and left with words that I absolutely had to be back no later than Tuesday. John, happy for any escape, agreed.

Over the years of hunting together, I'd sensed a growing loneliness hollowing inside John. His job kept him away from home in long stretches, and he admitted long ago that his wife had grown increasingly distant and cold. At a loss for some tenderness, he floundered about for a few years, searching for answers in places both healthy and unhealthy. Finally, weakened by the consuming emotional emptiness, he failed to stop some bad moments from happening and what he got in return, besides Jesus, was a crumbling family life and a parole officer named Bobo. An unforeseen consequence arose later; he couldn't have any access to or control of firearms for several years, including hunting seasons. If he wanted to hunt, he'd have to do it with bow and arrow.

The wind never eased as night grew old, a bad sign, and at 1:30 in the morning we pulled off the highway on the back side of a coulee and faced the truck into the wind. Besides being tired, the talk had gone past religion and past old hunting stories and had settled on things sad and melancholy. It was time to stop. We rolled out our bags in the bed of the truck, using the cab as a windbreak, and I slept well until John woke me just before dawn and reminded me that it was his birthday. The wind continued to blast and grayish clouds blew fast across the reddening sky. We stopped in Jordan at a Handi-mart and as I unloaded my munchies on the counter I overheard the owner lament to a local guy cupping an ancient green coffee mug that this was the second straight week of bad wind. Despite the dour weather John seemed energized, perhaps overly so, and anxious to be out hunting.

Forty minutes later we pulled into our spot and started to glass the flat. John found a little group of antelope right off the bat, bedded down in the middle of a prairie dog town. It was hard to get a good look at the buck in the spotting scope due to the wind, but he looked better than average and I told John I'd shoot him if we got the chance. Glassing the main creek bed a mile away, I spotted two mule deer bucks moving down the creek bank. One of the bucks was little, the other one a bit bigger, but still hard to tell how big at that distance. Deer season had just opened, but I had no interest in either of these deer this early in the year. The bucks abruptly about-faced and bounded back up the wash.

"Probably some other hunters up there that spooked them," I said.

"Naw," John said with his binoculars glued to his eyes. "They'll run up there and bed down by that big cottonwood tree."

"Somewhere up there," I said.

We agreed that a stalk on the antelope would require us to get in the creek wash anyway, so we drove closer and started to gear up. I clipped on my daypack and slung my rifle over my shoulder. John, awkward, looked at his bow and then at me.

"You can't kill anything without your weapon," I said flatly.

John seemed relieved at this and grabbed his bow. He started jabbering about how I shouldn't shoot that antelope until we had looked the country over real good and made sure a big hoss buck wasn't around. I didn't answer. Normally my trophy-infected self can be victimized by this type of talk, but the gusty wind and the short time frame left me unconflicted. Close to the side wash which lead to the antelope I stopped to bury some toilet paper. John moved ahead a safe distance and climbed out of the wash to glass.

A few minutes later I popped out of the wash on John's tracks. He was squatted down fifty yards ahead, frantically motioning me down, and kept flashing me with a peace sign and a fist. Two - zero? I eased down and John crawled back to me.

"Those two muley bucks are bedded 20 yards away from that cottonwood tree," John whispered. His eyes fairly danced. I noticed in amazement that it was the exact cottonwood that he had prophesied from the pickup.  "I waited so you could be here."

I promptly knelt on a cactus, grimaced, and began plucking the spines from my knee. I motioned him forward, rolled up, and watched. Squatting, John came to full draw, then eased up over the lip of the wash. The wind wavered his bow back and forth for a few seconds. John released. *Chunk!* I saw the little buck bound out the opposite side of the wash, but didn't see any sign of the bigger buck. I looked anxious for John's reaction, but his shoulders sagged and he turned and shook his head no.

"I must have shot over him. I heard the arrow hit in the dirt."

I finished plucking the cactus spines out of my knee and walked to the edge. I could see his arrow stuck in the ground. I focused on it with my binoculars.

"I think you got him," I said. "Your arrow has blood all over it."

"Probably just dirt."

We got to the arrow and picked it up. It was covered top to bottom in good lung blood. A cautious, disbelieving grin tugged at John's face, but there was to be no drama. The deer was piled up, dead, 75 yards up the wash.

The buck measured 24 inches wide, a single fork on one side and three points on the other with eye guards. A dandy bow kill, a perfect shot, and totally unexpected. A gift. No stranger to successful hunts and yet John bothered around back and forth as if unsure exactly what to do. Finally, he took a finger of the deer's blood and swabbed it down one cheek. We took lots of pictures from lots of angles and field dressed the buck. I deliberately drank my victory Mountain Dew. I congratulated him again on a great shot, and we both shook our heads in amazement at his calling of the exact tree they would be bedded under. John seemed vaguely relieved, as if the realization that he was still worthy of any kind of good luck somehow lifting a heavy weight. I took my time, breathing in the windy sage, aware enough to see that dead buck give something to John that all the people and all the pavement hadn't been able to give him for a very long time. A few moments of uncluttered joy.

An hour later I knelt behind the antelope buck and had John take my picture. Two nice bucks. Two different species. Two kinds of weapons. Two perfect shots. Two hours.

Impossible, really.

We stopped in Jordan to visit a friend of John's who is a taxidermist. We spent some time admiring the heads in his shop while John gushed out the events of our remarkable morning. Out of the blue the man innocently asked John how his other troubles were going. He was trying to be nice and seemed genuinely concerned, and I don't think he even saw how that single question sucked the light right out of John's eyes.

But the events of the day were too perfect, the spirit of the day too strong. John quickly revived. Even into the gusty wind, the ride for home was light and easy. We chatted and laughed, carefree, more and more amazed about the improbable events of the morning. John even fell asleep with his head against the window for a couple of hours. While he slept, I had the thought that from the moment we found his bloodied arrow that this day wasn't even about me anymore, that I was just a visitor to John's great birthday. Even so, I was swept along in the happiness of it and felt refreshed and content. I also knew the fleeting nature of such days, and we both knew that John's grim dogs had only temporarily been caged. I hoped the ride home would last a long time.

We stopped at the Town Pump in Lewistown to gas up. John bought a blank greeting card, glossy white with a dreamy western scene, and I knew he wanted to write a nice letter to his wife and perhaps extend the day's impossible good luck.

*****

Still in my work clothes, I turned my pickup off the highway and onto a gravel road, intending to pull over and change into my camo for a quick evening bowhunt. Before I could get stopped I spotted a whitetail doe in the trees just off the road. She was on public land and I had a doe tag for the area, so I drove past the deer until I was a safe distance out of sight. I snatched my bow from the back seat, strapped on my release, and pulled out an arrow, briefly inspecting the broadhead. Hastily I pulled my camo T-shirt right over my work shirt, put the truck in gear, and turned around.

The pickup rolled to where I'd seen the deer, just in time to see her casually flick her tail and feed over the top of the hill 60 yards away. When the truck stopped, I put it in park but left it running. Noiselessly, I opened the door and eased out, something not quite right, and carefully worked my bow past the steering wheel. Nocking the arrow, I thought about crawling under the barbed wire fence that paralleled the road. When I pushed on the top wire it gave about a foot so instead I swung my leg over, catching my pant leg on a barb in the process, nearly toppling me. The wire let out a loud screech as it released my leg.

I figured that was that, but sat still for a minute or two to let things quiet down and stalked up the hill anyway. Peering over the hill, I found the doe nibbling at a tangle of brush a mere thirty yards away, completely unconcerned. I ducked back to prepare for the shot and my blood went cold when I saw my release dangling uselessly off the wrong wrist.

*What an idiot!*

I crouched down and thumbed the velcro strap on the release as silently as I could and switched arms, breathing a couple of times afterwards to settle myself down.

I peeked over the hill again, certain now the doe would be gone. Not only was she still there, she had actually moved a few yards closer and offered an even better shot. Unbelievable. The arrow flew perfect and the doe ran about fifty yards and piled up within view, a bowhunting rarity. Pleased, I knelt beside her, patting her thick shoulder, admiring her sleekness, and I knew I had done nothing whatsoever to deserve her.

*****

It was plain to see that life had been hard on the old gent, and he reminded me of a gnarled old pinion growing out of bare stone high on the face of a windswept cliff. He bent strangely at the hips and a hoarse, raspy cough frequently heaved his chest. His fishing tackle was like his clothes, dirty and rough and barely functional. Just then, however, his snaggle-toothed face was arced in a broad grin.

Flopping at his feet was another beautiful rainbow trout, perhaps four or five pounds. Being early in the spring, the male trout was dark and hook-jawed, all fancied up in his spawning splendor. The old man unceremoniously whacked it over the head with a rock and slid it into a green five gallon bucket. Coughing, he hunched over his tackle box and re-baited.

I looked hopefully at my own line, hanging limp and drifting slightly in the easy breeze. The other rods my three small children were minding perched straight and undisturbed. Another guy farther down the bank sat silently, as if not to notice that this was the old man's third large rainbow in half an hour.

8

He casted into the cold waters of the reservoir, pulled up a tattered camp stool, and started nibbling on some mini-marshmallows he had found in his tackle box. My three year old boy Jacob, courageous after spotting the marshmallows, marched up to the old man and asked for some. Embarrassed, but happy for a chance to see what he was using for bait, I walked over to retreive my son.

"Got some nice ones," I said. "What are you using?"

"Spawn," he said, dribbling some of the rock-hard marshmallows into Jacob's cupped palms.

I looked in the bucket. Three fat, gorgeous rainbow trout curled in half-moons inside the bucket.

"Spawn, huh," I replied. "That's what we're using too."

"Wull, last week some guy pulled his limit right outta where yer blue pole is," he said. "I got two all day. Ain't no reason to it."

I couldn't help but notice his grin. I took Jacob by the hand and headed back to the poles. The old man stood suddenly off the camp stool, set the hook, and wrestled in another big fish. The other guy down the bank didn't even glance over.

Instantly, Jacob was back down there doing his Dennis-the-Menace and Mr. Wilson routine. I went to fetch him again.

"The next fish you catch, can I reel him in?" Jacob innocently asked.

I could see this pleased the old man no end, and he handed Jacob a couple more marshmallows. He winked at me, looking clownish with a ring of marshmallow dust around his lips.

"Why shore you can little fella."

"Hey Jake, we better get back to our own poles. You might have a fish right now," I tried.

"He ain't no trouble," the old man said. "Leave him be."

Jacob looked in the bucket. Even at three years of age, he knew where the action was. The dusty old man casted again and sat down. Jacob was asking him this and that as I walked back down the bank to check on the other two kids. I kept a watchful eye over to the old man, hearing his coarse cough and occasional laugh over the constant chirpings of my youngest son.

Thirty minutes and one more big fish later, the old man started packing his gear. I stood and went a third time to get Jacob. The old man looked visibly refreshed, a wide grin etched across his face. His life, I knew, hadn't always been with a wide grin.

"You got yerself a real live wire here," he said of Jacob. "Wull, looks like I got my limit, skunked y'all, and made a new friend to boot. I'd best be gettin' while the gettin's good." He grinned again, coughed deeply, and started lugging his gear to his rusty old sedan. Jacob followed behind, half dragging the fish bucket to the old man's car for him. He delivered the fish to the old man and bounded back down the bank. The old man tipped his hat at me and cackled out a laugh as he got into his car. I nodded back and twisted a grin for the old codger. Blue smoke poured out of his mufflerless sedan as he drove away.

I was genuinely happy for the old guy, the same way I'm happy when a 12 seed beats a 5 seed in the NCAA basketball tournament. He was king for a day. Fish, unlike most people, are no respecters of position or circumstance. The first can be last and the last can be first. Fish long enough and you'll see it yourself, and for whatever reason this day was the old man's day to be top dog.

We sat down there for a couple more hours and never did catch a fish.

*****

The alarm clock rang early. I flopped my arm out of the covers and hit the snooze. It rang again, and I talked myself into sleeping in a little. We already had an elk in the freezer and the deer rut hadn't really started yet. Anyway, the wind was up and what snow we had was old and crusty. I shut the alarm off and went back to sleep.

An hour later I got out of bed, full of regret for sleeping in, and decided it would be better late than never. The sun was fully up when I pulled out of the driveway. I drove into the mountains, hopeful that I might be lucky enough to participate in the old hunting story I'd heard many versions of but had never actually experienced. The story usually starts with "Well, we were a little late getting out of town..." and ends with a picture of a nice buck or bull loaded whole in the back of a pickup.

I gave it a good try and hunted hard for most of the day, feeling like the school kid who missed the bus and had to walk to school, tardier and tardier with every passing minute. In the afternoon it became apparent that I would never catch up to the day, and I lost hope and went home without seeing anything.

*****

On the second pass across the desert two track the headlights happened to catch a bit of reflector out in the sagebrush. I flicked the lights to high beam and hopped out to take a look. Sure enough, nailed to a broken post was a bent BLM sign that read "Willow Creek". I jumped back in the truck and turned right. Finally. The clock on the dashboard read 1:40 A.M. For two hours I had looked for this spot, driving out a cobweb of desert roads looking for that one stupid sign. An inauspicious beginning for sure.

I bounced up the broken road, the black night reducing my world to the reach of the headlights. My friend and salmon fishing buddy Reed had told me there would be a flat spot to camp about three miles up this road, just before the creek crossing. The original plan had been to get here yesterday, this morning at the latest, to set up camp and look for some elk before opening day. Delayed as usual by a flurry of last minute distractions and here I was, looking for a flat place in the road a mere five hours before opening morning. At least now I was out of cell range and had four full days of hunting in front of me. Four lucky, unexpected days. Lucky because folded in the front pocket of my daypack lay a limited entry bull elk permit and a photocopy of a BLM topo map with a circle highlighting a spring basin high in upper Willow Creek. I'd beaten one-in-eighty odds for the tag, and Reed sent me the map after telling me about seeing two huge bulls in that exact area a couple of years ago. And that's just what I wanted. A huge bull.

At the flat spot just before the creek crossing my headlights shined over two pickups and a camp trailer. Great. So far this wasn't looking good at all. What are the odds? Only thirty tags in a hunt area bigger than some states and I have company in this forsaken place.

*Maybe they aren't elk hunters...*

Well, it was too late to worry about it now. A quarter of a mile down the road I found a spot to pull off the road and stopped. Too tired to pitch the tent, I unrolled my pad and my bag in the bed of the pickup.

The sound of a truck passing by woke me and I jolted up to see a pickup disappear around the next corner in the road past me. I noticed with alarm the sky already growing light. It took me twenty minutes to load up my gear for the day, and I was so tired that I guzzled a big slam Mountain Dew for a little jolt. I started up the road on the 4-wheeler, not having a clue where to go but not wanting the other guys to get there first. After a mile or so I found the truck, and looking on the map seemed sure they were headed for the basin with the spring. I glassed into the distant basin and saw an elk move between a break in the trees but it was too far away to tell if it was a cow or a bull. I glassed around for the hunters but couldn't find them. I shifted the 4-wheeler and putted up the road. No sense in chasing those hunters around all day.

A half a mile farther I parked the quad in some willows and started hiking in the same direction as the basin but one ridge to the east. My legs felt leaden and slow. I pained for breath. After a half an hour I looked back, surprised at how little progress I'd made. Another half hour of tortuous uphill and I topped a little ridge and moved across a saddle. The basin with the spring opened into view from here, so I sat down under a fir snag and pulled off my daypack, ready to sit a while and glass. I was surprised at how horrible I felt and blamed it on the Mountain Dew, but when the magnified view of the basin registered I forgot all that. Elk were everywhere. Several bulls wandered back and forth through the cows and as my breathing slowed I could faintly make out their bugles. I glassed the other country available, but all the action was at the spring. Reed had certainly done his part.

I glassed for maybe fifteen minutes, watching the elk and looking for the hunters. The elk I saw in abundance, the hunters I did not. Maybe they had gone another direction. One thing for sure, I needed to get closer. I dropped straight off to the bottom and even with a basin full of elk on the other side, the hike up the opposite mountain didn't go any better. The thought came more than once that it would be better if I just puked and got it over with. I pushed on, and finally edged over the ridge and scurried to the shady side of a boulder the size of a Volkswagen. The elk were still way out of rifle range, but now I could hear the different bugles better and was positive that the hunters were in the mix, pushing the elk. Sure enough, a few minutes later my binoculars found two hunters in the timber.

One of the hunters had a rifle and a daypack, the other one carried only a big backpack. The guy in the backpack did all the bugling, and they moved through the trees toward the north rim of the mountain. Moving forward across the basin with the binoculars, I spotted several different bunches of elk filtering over the ridge. I counted at least seven branch antlered bulls, but no big boys. One nice six point and two cows double-backed high on the hill, escaping behind the hunters. I couldn't get much of a look at the bull's antlers but his body was huge and caked black in wallow mud.

The hunters eventually hit the ridge behind the elk and dropped off, still bugling constantly.

My hunting morning was over and my head was pounding. I rummaged through my daypack and found a bagel and an orange. Digging deeper, I came up with the Advil. The early October air had warmed considerably, and I didn't resist the urge to take off my boots and socks. After eating, I drank some water, and a genuine fatigue flooded over me. Using my daypack for a pillow, I stretched out and shut my eyes.

The crunching of footsteps woke me. The two hunters were coming back down the ridge.

"How's it going?" I muttered as I sat up, awkward at being caught sleeping in bare feet.

"Good," the guy with the rifle said, grinning.

"No shooting?" I asked.

"Lots of bulls but no takers. We're looking for a hog," the bugler said. "You elk hunting too?"

I nodded. I saw the flash of a smirk cross his face and I knew exactly what he was thinking; after all I'd been sleeping both times they'd passed me that morning.

"Did you see that black bull?" the hunter asked.

"Yeah, him and a couple of cows back-doored you while you were in the timber. Got out above you."

The two glanced at each other. I knew they didn't believe me.

"Well, good luck," they said, and turned to leave.

"Good luck to you too," I shrugged.

I lay back down, pulling my hat over my eyes, folding my arms over my chest. I found myself wanting to get up and run and catch the hunters and explain myself, how busy I'd been in the weeks before the hunt, how I had to leave late yesterday, that it was 2:00 in the morning before I got to sleep, that I had never been here before.

Instead I shut my eyes, breathing the air, and I suddenly knew why I felt so poor. I deserved it. I was out of sync and tired, and it obviously showed. I'd drug a dumpster of pavement garbage with me up here into the mountains. In my frenzy to simply *get* here I'd neglected to prepare to *be* here. I opened my eyes and looked at the wispy feathers of clouds suspended in the blue sky and noticed for the first time the breeze on my face. I watched an ant busy over my shirt sleeve, twitching, in constant motion, back and forth. I sat up on my elbows, the shadow of the granite peak above me still holding the bottom of the canyon in shade. The spring basin, which only three hours ago sang with the bugles of bull elk, now warmed before me sunlit, still, and quiet. I needed more than just rest. I needed to unsaddle myself of the pace of my life below. I had to slow down, to tune in, to match the rhythms of the mountains.

I spent most of the day in the shade of that rock.

*****

By the next afternoon I felt much better. In the morning I'd started hiking an hour before it got light up Dry Gulch, a secondary mark on Reed's map where I found myself without competition, and had looked over several small bull elk, a cow and bull moose, and a herd of six bighorn rams, two of which were full curl and gray. I got back to the road closure about noon, ate lunch, and slept soundly in the shade of my pickup for a couple of hours. I stopped in Leadore and called to see if Scott was still going to come and meet me tonight. He had unexpected troubles at work and couldn't make it until morning. Resisting the urge to check my voice mail, I hung up the phone and decided to go back to the spring basin and see if the hunters were still there.

I left my truck at a historical marker pull-out on the main highway and rode across the desert on the 4-wheeler. Warm air folded my hair back over my forehead and it felt good to be going so fast in the open air. The hunter's camp trailer was still there but the pickups were not. I drove on up the road and found their parking spot empty. With only three hours until dark and with no better options, I geared up and uncased my gun. I looked at the camera in the saddlebag of the 4-wheeler. Usually the camera goes in later, with the game bags, but I had a sudden notion and at the last minute packed it in the top of my daypack.

The hike up the ridge went much better than the day before. About half way up, I glassed a cow and a young bull moving amid the trees at the upper end of the basin. Good news. Forty minutes later, I eased under a big fir tree at the edge of the upper spring and sat down. I had barely rubbed out a comfortable spot under the tree with my rump when an elk bugle nearly parted my hair. I leaned forward to see a nice, square five-point bull standing in a wallow 80 yards away. I guessed him to be 3 years old, with long front tines, and on virtually any other occasion he would have swiftly been venison. The bull caught my motion when I leaned forward and we had a five minute stare off. He got a little nervous and moved out of the wallow, ambling across the hill in slam dunk rifle range. It was too soon to use this precious tag on that young bull but I couldn't help thinking that I would regret letting him go.

Several bulls were bugling back and forth and with about half an hour of daylight left I heard a new bugle, throaty and full, below me and at the other end of the basin. It sounded like something that needed to be investigated and there wasn't much daylight left. I stood up and cautiously walked along the edge of the timber. Right off the bat I saw elk legs in the trees above me, forty yards away. A cow, frozen in place, and staring right at me. Without stopping I just kept moving slow, not even looking at the elk. She let me get past her and I heard her crash off behind me. Whew. I knew I'd just dodged a major bullet.

I heard the throaty bugle in uneven but fairly regular intervals. Through the limbs I began to see scatterings of elk filtering in and out a few hundred yards below me. About a dozen cows and calves, but the only bull I had seen down there so far was a spike. It couldn't be that little spike making that big bugle. I needed to get past a little clump of aspens for the view to open up a little and when it did the heavens opened up with it.

Below, knee-deep in a bog, a huge bull threw his head back and bugled the big bugle. Cows and calves mingled around and the big bull moved decisively back and forth along the edge, keeping them below him. His main beams were flank scratchers with nice whale tails, a clean six point, and only three hundred yards away. I fought the urge to just shoot. The bull was in a good spot, and so was I. I could get closer. Edging forward a single step at a time, glassing between every step, I closed the gap to a little over 200 yards. A cow finally swiveled her head up the hill and pegged me. It was time.

I trotted ahead to the nearest aspen tree, laid the rifle over a branch, and flicked the safety off. The big bull popped into view in the scope, the crosshairs perfect on his chest. He turned slightly away, still unaware, but now leaving me with a bad angle. I glanced at the cow. She was leaving. I waited. The bull turned back a bit, and then broadside. The gun went off when it should have and the big elk dropped in his tracks, pole-axed with a broken back. Elk stampeded everywhere, including another great big bull above me that I hadn't seen. I reloaded my single shot rifle and kept my focus until I was at the enormous bull's side.

He was a splendid, big-bodied herd bull, his long, magnificent antlers with six mirror image points per side. His main beams looked to be well over 50 inches, his daggers about 20. He reeked of that peculiar smell of elk rut, and I breathed it in deeply as I circled him four or five times, awestruck at every angle. He had even died in some fairly level scrub at the edge of a bog, a perfect place to gut and quarter him.

The remarkable circumstances and gathering darkness gave the whole perfect scene a dreamy, surreal texture, and for quite a while an honest-to-goodness sense of *deja vu* swallowed me up and made me think that I'd been here before. From the minute I put the camera in my daypack, this entire hunt had been a perfect string of bugling elk, close calls, and good luck. It was as if I'd been dropped right into the middle of a happy, big bull high definition dream, or like I had been granted a cosmic wish in which all the grand and fortunate events of the hunt had happened just so simply because I had wanted them to. It was almost impossible to believe that it was only yesterday morning that I had felt so poorly, so tired, hoping to puke, resting in the shade of a rock. But that was yesterday. On this day, I had found my mountain balance, and had been deeply and uniquely connected to the entire day. Completely in touch. Wholly in tune. Totally in rhythm.

After exposing a roll of film, I cleaned the magnificent bull by flashlight, laying a sweaty shirt over him to keep the coyotes off until me and Dad could come back in the morning with the horses. I put the flashlight in my pocket and walked off the hill in the dark, as free as I will ever be in this life and light, feeling like I could walk all night, like I could walk right off the hill and into the gathering stars if I wanted to.

# ANTUS LOPUS

*"The way of a fool is right in his own eyes" Proverbs 12:15*

By the time I graduated from college in 1987, my wife and I already had one kid on the ground and another on the way, so there were plenty of diversions for the starvation-grade salary I was earning as a fledgling life insurance agent. In fact, the cash flow looked like a dusty jigsaw puzzle of baked clay long before the diversions ran out. One summer evening I was out at my good friend Doug Larsen's house trying to pester him into buying some life insurance. He deflected the issue by asking if I was going to get in on the early season archery antelope hunt near Idaho Falls in the management units bordering the Site. Should be a piece of cake, that's what he told me. Lots of antelope. Eating the farmer's crops like a blizzard of prong-horned grasshoppers. Big bucks too. Pope and Youngers. How hard could it be? The old timers almost wiped them out of the West by putting a white hanky on a stick and luring them into range, for crying out loud.

I got excited, that's for sure. Driving home I was daydreaming about being on the cover of a hunting magazine with my record book antelope when I happened to see the blank insurance application on the passenger seat. Cold, hard reality set in. I needed arrows and broadheads, an antelope tag, and a few tanks of gas. Thanks to a timely Christmas present the year before, I already had a bow. A PSE Gamesport, 1986's bottom of the line compound bow which was long and heavy but made up for it by shooting slow. The money for the rest of it seemed impossible. But I was young and ambitious and I lived in Idaho Falls, as in Idaho Falls *America*, and so after three or four all-nighters gathering nightcrawlers and selling them to a bait company I had an antelope tag and six pawn-shop arrows and the cheapest broadheads money could buy.

The United States government owns a huge swath of high desert in southern Idaho for the purpose of nuclear research and development. Ironically, Idaho has been the home to many Navy personnel over the years, seamen training to operate nuclear submarines out in the sagebrush and lava rock, hundreds of miles from an actual ocean. At the time it was called the Idaho National Engineering Laboratory, or INEL, but most people just called it the Site. Due to the nature of atomic research, access to the Site was strictly limited. Most of the workers at the Site bussed to and from work in the big silver and yellow Site busses, security badges dangling off their shirts. Absolutely no hunting or trespassing was allowed beyond the clearly posted boundary, and because of this secure habitat the pronghorn antelope population had exploded, and agricultural landowners whose crops were being mauled demanded some relief. The result was the archery antelope season.

So under the stars of a mid-August opening morning Troy Thompson, Doug Larsen and I rattled out to the desert in Troy's old blue Ford pickup to kill us a few Pope and Young antelope. How hard could it be to get an arrow into a dumb old desert goat? We sported ourselves with manly talk of spot-and-stalk as the skyline turned orange, laughing at Troy when he tried to hit the high notes with Whitney Houston on the radio. Trying to show off my new college degree, I asked if anybody knew the Latin name for the pronghorn antelope. Nobody did.

"*Antus lopus*," I replied matter of factly.

"We're so proud of you," Troy mocked.

We pulled off the gravel road just as daylight was breaking and quickly spotted some antelope, but they spotted us just as quickly and left a little dust trail marking their safe retreat into the Site. Undeterred, we spotted and stalked the rest of that day and most of the next. We actually got close once, but that was when we crested a rise in the pickup and a few antelope were standing in the faint two-track road ahead. The white hairs on their rumps flared and even before the truck skidded to a sideways stop and we peeled our faces off the inside of the windshield they were up on a little ridge, running parallel with the road. Troy hit the gas and the antelope sped up, running alongside us up the road. It was plain they wanted to cross over. Once or twice Troy had the old Ford airborne, and as the Pepsi jostled out of our cans and we braced our heads from hitting the roof, I glanced over at the speedometer. It was bouncing around 50. The antelope finally darted in front of us, little rooster tails of dust kicking up in the road under their feet as they peeled away and kept running out of sight.

This gave us an idea. We went trolling for antelope. For you younger readers, be assured that this was in the days before bowhunter safety classes and back when "ethics" was some sort of delicious Greek food made with spiced meat. Do not attempt this method of hunting antelope. Anyway, I drove while Troy and Doug braced themselves with arrows nocked in the back of the pickup. Before long I was easing the old Ford up to a little band of antelope which had one really nice buck in it. They jittered and pranced and then broke and ran. I floored it. True to form, the antelope raced along side, but I tried to keep the truck close enough so that they couldn't cross in front of us. We were going alarmingly fast and I peeked in the rear view mirror to see Doug's legs bent and his feet splayed wide against the fender wells, his knees absorbing the road like two jackhammers. I kept glancing from the rear view mirror to the road, and in frames I saw Doug draw his bow and swing it on the antelope racing along only twenty yards out. Once again the speedometer was nearing 50. When he shot, the arrow planed in the cross wind and looped cartoonishly, landing far, far behind the antelope.

A few days later, Doug and I were on the grass behind my apartment with a refrigerator box, some spray paint, and a couple of razor cutters. We had noticed that the antelope that came off the Site onto the croplands seemed perfectly content to let cattle graze within feet of them. We had heard of decoying antelope, and so we were doing our best to morph the box into a Hereford cow. Somewhere along the line my wife Kim showed up, peeking over our shoulders to see what we were up to. I suddenly flushed with the feeling you got when you were a kid and you were in the backyard taking the motor off the lawnmower to build a go-cart and your dad came out of nowhere and asked what you were doing. I answered before the question could be asked.

"We're making a cow," I said flatly.

"Oh," she replied just as flatly. "Making a cow. Sure."

Doug never looked up but was grinning ear to ear. Kim rolled her eyes, perhaps wondering why her college educated husband couldn't find something better to do with an afternoon than carve a cow out of a refrigerator box. Packing our toddler on her hip, she turned and went inside.

"I'll explain it to her later," I said to no one in particular.

The next morning found us at the corner of a huge pasture that bordered the Site. Antelope could already be seen in with the cows. By now we had respect for the spotting-scope vision of antelope, so we crept low and out of sight until we were in the bottom of a small ditch. We grinned at each other as we unfolded the cardboard cow and propped it up in front of us, crawling along behind, one hand on our bows and the other on the little handles we had so brilliantly devised to keep the cow upright. I peeked around the rump roast. So far so good.

We made it another hundred yards or so before even the cows ran off. The antelope were already long gone.

As the season wore on we began to notice things about *antus lopus*. The old timer who said you could put a hanky on a stick and lure them into range was definitely not archery hunting with a PSE Gamesport, and in a drunken stupor must have confused antelope with snow geese. Antelope have two primary defenses, ten-power eyesight and speed. They like to cross fences in the same places, will hardly ever jump a fence, and will walk a fence line a long ways to get to a crossing. They'll move at any time of the day. They'll drink at any time of the day. If they see you first, they're gone. If you hear an alarm wheeze, which sounds like a whitetail's, they're gone. Under the cover of darkness they seem much less skittish. We tried to take advantage of our hard-earned knowledge.

We sat on water holes. We sat on fence crossings. We found better terrain to stalk. Mostly we failed, but one morning as we drove out we noticed a herd of antelope bunched up in a corner of a hay field along a farm road. From a long ways away, Troy slowed the truck to a snail's pace, and Doug slipped out of the cab on the opposite side of the truck. Trotting along using the truck for cover, he pulled an arrow from his quiver and nocked it. When he was directly across from the antelope, he ducked into the ditch along the road while we kept going in the truck. The antelope riveted on the truck and got real nervous but stayed put. Doug drew his bow and shot. A clean miss, but a legitimate chance, and with that shot a gush of helium filled our flattened balloons of hope.

Doug put his bow in the back of the truck, and went into the field to look for his arrow. The antelope ran to the far opposite corner of the field and Troy and I drove off, hoping for a repeat performance. However, *antus lopus* learns quickly and before the truck even got close the antelope bolted back toward the original corner of the field. I shall long remember the sight of Doug Larsen crouched in the hay field, the antelope pouring point-blank around him like river water around a rock, holding his useless arrow in his hand, his now useless bow clattering in the back of a pickup a half a mile away. Doug hurled his arrow and many new Latin names at *antus lopus* on that day, blended creatively with some classic one-syllable American English.

Finally we dug pit blinds. Right on the border of the Site and on the edges of the hay fields. We dug them about three feet deep and lined them with a couple of layers of straw bales, leaving some shooting windows open. We scavenged up some sagebrush to stick in the bales to cover the movement of our bows. In the dark of early morning we'd slip into our blinds and wait for the sun to come up. A couple of blown opportunities taught us to let the antelope walk past the blind and into the field before drawing our bows. I went out by myself one morning, jumped into my blind, propped up the sagebrush, and fell asleep. The season was nearly over, and I was worn out from the many early mornings.

When I woke up, I scanned the edge of the desert with my binoculars. Poking along single file were two or three does and a huge buck that we'd seen out on the Site a few times but had never had a chance at. They were still three hundred yards out, but they were coming perfect. I tried to quiet the blood pounding in my ears, but my breath came short and raspy. I nocked an arrow and propped my bow toward the anticipated shooting lane. Every so often I'd peek up. They were still coming. It didn't help that the magazine picture I had visualized a few weeks before flashed back in my head. My knees went sodden.

*"Come on Chris,"* I told myself. *"Get it together. Breathe. Breathe."*

When the antelope were about a hundred yards from my blind, the does broke and trotted right past my blind and into the field. I held my breath, but the black-faced buck stood back, frozen in the sagebrush. He was huge! I guessed him conservatively at sixteen inches. A Pope and Younger for sure. Maybe the Idaho State Record Archery Antelope! But he just stood there, facing the blind. I figured I must be busted and considered briefly a shot at one of the does. All of a sudden the buck started coming. I tensed up, slowly bracing myself for the shot. He trotted by the blind at ten yards and turned broadside in the hay field at about thirty. He placidly grazed as I drew my bow. I drew my bow! By the gods, I drew my bow!

Permanently etched in my mind is the sight picture of that gigantic antelope buck, broadside, framed by a window of straw bales, my broadhead sitting on the arrow rest, pointed at his heart. My thirty yard pin settled behind his shoulder and I released, the path of the arrow in slow motion, flying perfect, then dropping and cutting a swath of air two or three inches below his brisket. Oh no! I choked! The antelope blew out and ran past the horizon. I stood up and watched them leave, my stomach turning over. I almost vomited. It seemed like nothing in my whole life had been over so fast. I had calmed down a little on the drive home, but still had to swallow a knot in my throat when I told Kim about my missed buck.

A couple of mornings later, right near the end of the season, I went out for one last chance. I slipped confidently up the road in the dark to my blind. I felt good. A little extra sleep and the fact that the field had been rested for a couple days had my hopes high. I hopped inside the blind as usual, unaware that five or six sage grouse had chosen my pit to roost for the night. Simultaneous to my jumping in, they flew out. So sudden and shocking was my fright that I very nearly changed the camo pattern on the seat of my hunting pants. I had no choice but to consider this good luck.

When the sun came up there wasn't an antelope in sight. I waited for a couple of hours and finally a small herd appeared on the heat-waved desert horizon. I could see right off they were going to be too far north, but I kept a vigilant eye out anyway. A few minutes later, I saw a doe antelope skylined two hundred yards to the north on the top of an irrigation ditch. I kept thinking she'd lead the herd into the hay field but they never showed. I was just about to stand up to get a good look when I saw the tops of the antelope's ears a mere three feet from my blind. The ears swayed back and forth, getting larger, until the doe literally stuck her head inside my blind. I crouched frozen on the back wall. There was a look of curiosity on her face for a second or two and then horrible recognition and her eyes rolled wild and she almost turned inside out, scorching across the desert without slowing down until she was out of sight. Twice that morning I had game inside the blind with me and I still had to eat peanut butter and jelly.

I didn't have any other chances, but one day I arrived at the insurance office and the secretary brought in a pink message note. This was unusual, as I had been hunting a lot more than I'd been selling insurance. The time and date were meticulously stenciled and the box marked urgent was crossed.

"Ten inch buck *antus lopus*. Blind by the gravel pit. Have a nice day. Doug."

A few days later Doug brought in the pictures of his buck and showed me his new elk call. All you had to do was bugle on that call during the rut and the bulls would come right in. Should be a piece of cake. That's what he said. The old timers used to have big bulls charge in on the gallop just by blowing on a willow whistle or a piece of fluted copper pipe, for crying out loud.

Not long after that I quit selling insurance.

## OUTA-STATERS

*"Thou shalt neither vex a stranger, nor oppress him..." Exodus 22:21*

Dave and I bumped down the remote jeep trail in his pickup, chained up on all four, when we saw two hunters in front of us walking down the road. As we approached, the guy wearing a big black cowboy hat motioned for us to stop. Assuming that they might need some help, we obliged. Dave stopped the truck and I rolled down my window as the cowboy hat approached.

"Howdee partner!" the young man's face under the black hat drawled unconvincingly. I glanced over at Dave.

"Oh boy," he whispered, rolling his eyes.

Although bone weary from two and a half days of packing out elk pieces on my back, I refused to pass this up.

"Well, howdee to you - or should I say y'all! Bee-you-tee-ful day for a walk down the road, ain't it boys? Where y'all from?"

I could practically hear Dave biting his lip.

"Michigan. Say, you wouldn't know where the elk are around here, would you?"

"Michigan, huh! Wow, that's a long ways from here, up by Maine somewhere, ain't it?" Before he could answer I kept going, "As for elk, I know where two bulls are right this minute."

"Really? Where?" The man's face lit up a bit.

"Right here in the back of this truck under the topper! Killed them three days ago, and been until just now packing them out!"

"Can we see?" the other guy asked.

"Oh boy," Dave whispered again.

We got out of the truck to a clatter of questions. "Where were they?" "How many did you see?" "Were there any other bulls?" "How far back were you?"

Dave squeaked open the topper and we showed them the bedraggled quarters of elk tossed together on a blue tarp with the two sets of smallish antlers on top. The two hunters each held a set of horns like they had just been handed the Holy Grail, and their whole sad story spilled out. They'd saved up for a couple of years applying for permits, but when they drew their tags for Montana, they still couldn't afford an outfitter. A neighbor they knew in Michigan had been on a guided hunt in the area years ago and drew them a map, practically assuring them that there was an elk behind every tree. They had been hunting in Montana for a full week and hadn't even seen an elk. They'd seen lots of tracks down by the road, and had tried walking the road the past two days without success. Besides that, Mr. Black Cowboy Hat's feet were killing him, and I looked down to see him in brand new, vibram-soled packer boots, not exactly the best choice for mountain hiking. To be honest, I began to feel a bit charitable towards the two since we already had our elk and it was Sunday and they truly seemed totally lost. Just then Dave, very uncharacteristically, broke loose.

"Dark Hollow," he said simply.

"Oh, I think we were there a couple of days ago."

"How about the Meadow Fork?" Dave asked.

"Yeah, I think we tried that too. Same day as Dark Hollow."

Dave glanced at me again. You couldn't take a helicopter and hunt Dark Hollow and the Meadow Fork in the same day. I smiled and shrugged. We'd tried, but you can't help the helpless. Shutting the topper, I faced these two eager but somewhat clueless hunters and offered the best advice I could possibly give them, or any other hunters of elk in the big mountains for that matter.

"If you really want to kill an elk in these mountains, here's what you do."

I paused for effect.

"Get up two hours before light and start hiking uphill. Keep hiking uphill clear to the top, until the only way you can go in any direction is back down. Then stay up in country like that and hunt the thickest timber you can find the rest of the day."

"How come there are all these tracks down here in the road then, if the elk are clear up on top?" Mr. Black Cowboy Hat countered, clearly smelling a rat.

"Elk are wandering critters, especially during hunting season. They move all over, mostly at night, and remember that elk tracks only tell you where an elk has been, not where he is. Them elk are on top alright," Dave explained. "It will take two feet of snow to get them to come out of there and stay out."

"What do you do if you shoot one clear up there?" the other one asked.

I tipped my head toward the elk quarters and the tattered and bloody pack frames in the back of the truck.

"Four hours to kill them. Two and a half days to get them out," I said.

The reality of the task in front of them began to settle across their grim faces. It was plain that their neighbor's sunny description of elk hunting in Montana had built up a very false sense of optimism, and I wasn't sure if we had done them a favor by helping out. But in those few moments we had told them the truth, more than they deserved, and given them information that had taken Dave and me many years of hunting the area to learn. They started to discuss between themselves as we climbed back in the truck and Dave started creaking down the road.

"Good luck fellas," I said.

Dave and I got back in the truck and rolled up the windows.

"Damned outa-staters," Dave growled.


*****


The year before we met the Michigan guys, I was elk hunting with Dave in a different area, driving up another mountain road right at the crack of first light. We rounded a corner and spotted a herd of elk scattered across the snowy slope of a basin high above the road. We parked the truck and made a quick plan. I went straight up the slide to the right, Dave circled around to the left. The elk came my direction, although I barely made it to the saddle on the ridgetop in time.

Lucky for me and unlucky for him, the five point bull in the bunch died on a steep, snow-covered hillside directly above my '79 International Scout II. Thanks to the steep pitch of the hill and the snow, I was able to drag him out whole to the creek bottom. I backed the Scout as close to the creek as I could and by attaching every piece of rope and chain that I had to the bumper, I had just barely enough line to get a knot around his antlers. I carefully pulled him through the creek and up to the parking spot. A five point bull elk out of the mountains. The same day. Whole. Life was good!

Dave had a cow tag for the area, and I knew he would give chase to the elk until either Jesus came again or complete darkness fell, especially with the fresh tracking snow. I had some time to kill, so I shuffled all our gear and cleared out a spot in the back of the Scout for a nap. I took special care to open the area near the back plate window on the drivers' side, since that was the side the sun was shining on. Quite pleased with myself and the great good fortune of the morning, I crawled in the back, placed my head on my coat for a pillow, turned my face so it was warming in the window, and went to sleep.

I suddenly opened my eyes to see a strange and bearded face inches from my own, looking at me directly through the window. I bolted awake, gasped a naughty word, and then quickly repented. I wondered momentarily if indeed Jesus had returned again.

"Is that your elk?" the man asked, pointing at my bull. Now that I was awake he reduced quickly from Deity to damned outa-stater.

"What elk?" I said flatly.

"That dead one right there. He's a dandy."

"Oh that one. Yeah, that's my elk. Shot him this morning."

"Right here, by the road?" he asked incredulously.

"Well, not exactly right by the road."

"Where did you get him?" he persisted.

"Once in the shoulder, once through the chest," I deflected.

"No, what I mean is..."

"Up on top." I said, pointing to the bloody drag slide off the hill in the snow. "Where you from?" I asked, changing the subject.

"Pennsylvania."

"Pennsylvania. Wow, that's a long way from here. Where vampires come from, right? Down by Florida? Anyway, how's the hunting been?"

"There's eight of us in the lodge," he continued, unfazed, and there was a sincerity in his smile that I found quite engaging. "All of us out West for our first elk hunt. Actually, this is my first big game hunt of any kind. I usually hunt birds with my dogs. Anyway, we've had good mule deer hunting but no elk yet. I got a four pointer and my brother got a four pointer and my friend got a...an....a...what do you call it...a pronghorn buck."

"An antelope, up this high?" I questioned.

"No, it's a... a..." He seemed at a loss for words, and finally he pointed both his index fingers above his ears.

"Oh, a spike!" I said.

"Yeah, a spike. That's it," he replied, and he smiled again with his whole face. I suddenly got a better picture of his four pointer.

"Your deer, did it have four points on each side?"

"No, that'd be an eight pointer. Mine had two long points on each side," he explained proudly.

"Here in Montana a buck like that is a two point, or you can call it a forked-horn."

"OK, well then he's a forked horn," he said. "Thanks for that."

We chatted a minute longer, and I wished him good luck. He congratulated me again on my elk and disappeared down the road. I was surprised a few minutes later to see him up on the hill, and I watched as he gradually backtracked the drag slide of my elk clear to the top of the ridge. Then he followed my bull's tracks back to the saddle, and I watched him through the binoculars as he poked around in the morning's elk tracks, sorting them out, and then he disappeared over the top into the timber beyond in the direction the elk had gone.

*Atta boy. Good luck, buddy.*

And from that very moment I thought of that guy as a hunter, not just some clueless outa-stater from Pennsylvania.

*****

A couple of friends of mine from Utah who I played football with in college drew Montana deer tags and came up hunting a few years back. I like to refer to my friends from Utah as "U-tards", and these guys are no exception. Dan Pedersen is the funniest human being I know, and more than once I have come home from a hunting trip with him and my stomach muscles are the sorest part of my body from laughing so much. He is goliath of a man, a former defensive tackle whose weight shift has been more dramatic than most. His hunter orange vest strings across his bulk like a halter top, and he reported with some satisfaction that he was down to a rather svelte 340 pounds for the hunt.

Troy Fullmer played linebacker in the old days, has bounced around in various sales careers, and has forgotten more about motivational speaking and positive mental attitude than most of us will ever learn. One evening, hopefully due to serious sleep deprivation, he alarmed the whole family with a bizarre rendition of the song "Halloween Cat", acting out the song with an improvised dance so freakish that it actually made the song pretty darned spooky. Dan's fourteen year old son Easton also joined us.

Dan and Easton were hoping for a whitetail buck, while Troy had a mule deer permit for an area close to town. One evening, I took Troy up to a place that is a family honey hole and he shot a nice buck right on top. The sun wasn't fully set, leaving me a little more hunting time. I was glassing and poking along, looking for deer, as Troy kept a distance behind dragging his buck with him. This seemed to be working well until the face of the mountain went quite steep, and suddenly I heard a big commotion on the hill above and behind me.

I turned just in time to see the dead deer bobsledding by on its back, front legs open, back legs splayed wide, sliding down the hill head first. On top of the deer, in what appeared to be a carnally compromising position, was Troy. His eyes were wide and he had his arms clutched around the buck's neck. The barrel from his gun kept bonking him on the back of the head as they slid another twenty feet or so past me before piling up against a tree.

I hooted and hollered, "Ride 'em cowboy! Give him the spurs! Yee-Haw!"

Later, in the pickup on the way home, Troy told me what happened. The deer slid up against an old stump and got stuck. He tried to pull it free but it wouldn't budge. He then went directly below the buck and pulled. Again nothing happened. He pulled harder and then even harder and then the deer came free all at once, spilling down the hill and taking Troy's feet out from under him in the process. Rather than fall down the mountain by himself, he latched onto the deer as it careened under him, ending up in the bestial embrace that I knew Troy had not heard the last of.

I waited until the dinner table, with everyone gathered together, and recounted the whole story. The table erupted in laughter at the thought of the Halloween Cat rump-riding the poor dead buck down the hill. I waited for the table to quiet a little.

"Hey Troy," I said in the tone of voice I use to give my children profound advice. "You know the deal with you on top of that buck? That's not what I meant when I asked if you were going to 'mount' that deer you silly U-tard. What I meant was, are you going to take it to the taxidermist?"

To his credit, Troy just smiled and took it like a man.

*****

I've been in line with my small kids for 47 minutes to ride the teacups. A voice comes over the loudspeaker.

"Disneyland is now at maximum capacity. No more visitors will be allowed into the park except as other park visitors leave. If you leave the park, you will only be allowed to return as other visitors leave. Thank you."

I turned to the sun-tanned soccer mom behind me.

"I wonder what 'maximum capacity' is? A million?"

She averted my gaze and parked her little girl behind her legs and stared over the top of the line as if she'd just recognized me as Hannibal Lecter. My kids and I had a great ride on the teacups, probably about two and a half minutes worth, and by then I needed a drink. I found a little kiosk and got in line.

"How's it going?" I said to the guy behind me.

He glanced at me, startled. "Fine."

But the word leaked out, probably from habit, and then he regained his composure and never looked anywhere near my direction again. In a few minutes I got to the front of the line.

"A large Diet Coke please."

"Four bucks," the attendant said.

"No, I only want one," I replied, only half joking.

No smile, no grin. Annoyed, he held up his palm and motioned with his fingers for the money, quickly handed me my soda, and looked over my head to the next customer. For a place that is supposed to be all about fun, there sure seemed to be a bunch of grouchy people around. And four bucks for a Diet Coke? What's fun about that?

My wife Kim, who grew up in California and who has a whole childhood crammed with warm fuzzy memories of Disneyland, took a couple of the kids to a line to get on a ride and I took the other two to a different line. The lines looked about even starting out, but she got through her line and was halfway through the next before I even made it through the first ride. I kept a sharp eye out for any teenaged punks who might be butting in line, but everybody just moved forward in this slow and rhythmic death shuffle. There seemed to be inside this Magic Kingdom some Magic Rule of Lines that I hadn't read about in the brochure. So I shuffled with the rest, somehow losing ground, and occasionally looking behind me and saying "How's it going?" to somebody, just to scare them.

A parade started, about the fourteenth one of the day, and Kim wanted to get close and take a picture. She grabbed two kids by the hands and I grabbed the other two, but in about a minute she was forty jam-packed people in front of me. I must not have the Magic Rule of Crowds going for me either.

Late in the day, going through the $60.00 sweatshirts in a gift shop, I finally found some magic in the Magic Kingdom.

"How's it going?" I asked a guy monotonously.

"Are you kidding me? This place sucks!" came the instant and confident reply.

It was my turn to be startled. A guy in his twenties was sitting on a bench looking like he had just had his toes amputated.

"Where are you from?" I asked.

"Wyoming."

I had found a brother. We chatted for a few minutes before his wife snapped her fingers for the second time.

"Take it easy," he said, disappearing into the masses.

Leaving the park, I found out that the maximum capacity of Disneyland at the time was 80,000 people. That is just about ten percent of the entire population of my home state of Montana, all crammed into a theme park not much bigger than a Bitterroot hobby farm, having fun with pretend mice and pretend ducks and elves and fairies and fake dwarfs, sipping on very real $4.00 Diet Cokes, making sure never to directly look at anyone, standing in lines with more people than live in my county, just to ride a properly insured ride in a properly restrained way. What a blast!

While everyone else in the family was having a great time, the Disneyland Christmas Vacation of a Lifetme as it were, I spent the day completely out of my element. I felt compressed and claustrophobic, and by the end of the day I was inexplicably exhausted. I was actually looking forward to seeing Winnemucca, Nevada again.

Once we got outside the gate, it took me a minute to get my bearings. Mmmm. Let's see, now where did I park the car...

# OUT OF THE CLOSET

*"for the Lord seeth not as man seeth; for man looketh on the outward appearance, but the Lord looketh on the heart." 1 Samuel 16:7*

I suppose the best thing to do right here is to simply man up, put my big boy pants on, and just come out with it. After years of confusion and experimentation, the time has come for me to come out of the closet, so to speak, and say this:

I don't believe in camo. I don't wear camo. I don't buy camo. I am, at long last, camo free!

I know, I know. Such sacrilege and blasphemy is going to be hard to take among the brotherhood of bowhunters, but before there is a stampede to flog me to death with your grunt tubes, hear me out. Like most journeys of intimate and personal self-discovery, this one had innocent beginnings and an unpredictable outcome. But, unlike most journeys of intimate and personal self discovery, I have photographic proof that I am willing to share.

Believe it or not, this whole thing started with a simple birthday present that cost less than $20.00. Before I opened that gift, I had camo that looked like tree bark, camo for the desert, camo for the ridges, camo for the river bottom, snow camo, and camo with computer sophistry. At a sportsman's show I very nearly bought a suit of camo that would have made me look like a giant mop. I pondered a camo system where a hunter could wear a leafy top and tree bark pants and just go out in the woods and stand wherever he wanted to. I wore a camo tie to church, bought Kim a camo nighty, and fixed things with camo duct tape. One winter when I drove by a frozen lake and most of the ice fishermen were wearing camo I never gave it a second thought.

All that changed back in 2007 on the day before I left for my first ever guided caribou hunt, which also happened to be my birthday. I sat on the couch and unwrapped the gift from Kim that would turn out to be the Holy Grail of all birthday presents. A quilted dark green plaid flannel zipper jacket with a gray sweat hood in extra-large tall. The jacket was made in Cambodia for Field and Stream and sold at Costco for $18.99. According to information taken from the actual tag on the jacket, which is sophisticated enough to be printed in two languages, this jacket is made up of 180% cotton, 100% nylon, and 120% polyester. For you math challenged readers, that adds up to a whopping 400%. Obviously this was no ordinary garment, and it is definitely not camouflage in any way, shape, or form.

The next day I flew out to Canada, and when I stepped off the plane wearing my green plaid jacket our camp guide Lou pulled me aside. Understand that this Lou is one tough and hard man, a French-Canadian that only uses one explicit adjective when he speaks English. Actually he creatively uses variations of that same word as noun, verb, adjective, and adverb. Lou told us that earlier in his life he had been sentenced to 18 months in prison for beating up a guy who had stolen one of his guns, and reported with a sense of grim satisfaction that he had to do all 18 months too. No time off for good behavior, so I was unsure what he was after.

"Is that your camo?" he asked me.

"Yep."

"Are you going to wear it hunting?"

"If it's not raining," I answered cautiously.

He looked into the heavens as if he were seeing a vision. "I never thought I'd see the day when an American got off that plane without $600.00 worth of brand new camo on."

"Hey," I said, somewhat offended. "This is brand new."

I killed the first caribou in camp wearing the plaid jacket the next day, a dandy double-shovel bull, and hung my second tag on another nice bull a few days later.

About a week after I got home from Canada, I was itching to get out bowhunting for elk, and my sons had reported seeing a nice bull and a few cows up in a basin not too far from home.

"I'm going to go up and kill that bull today," I told Jake and Devin early one morning as they were heading out the door for early morning seminary.

"Yeah, sure you are Dad," one of them said. "And while you're at it you might as well go out and win the Heisman Trophy." They were still snickering as I zipped up my plaid jacket and drove away.

Five hours later I was standing over the big bull trying to get a good self-timer photo. Just after sunrise I spotted the elk out in the flats a long ways below the timbered basin but assumed that they would end up there before the day got too hot. I set up on the ground in a little string of brush and waited three hours for the elk to get to me. Problem was, all the elk crossed about 100 yards below me, the bull the last in line. By now a marginal crosswind was wafting toward the cows and I had little to lose at this point, so I gave him a short little spikish-sounding squeak on my bugle. I rarely bugle at elk anymore, but when I do I like to try to sound like a vulnerable little sissy. The bull instantly threw his head back and ripped out an enormous non-sissy bugle and came in so fast that I barely got turned around and my bow drawn before he popped into the open at 35 yards. I saw my arrow hit him a couple inches high of perfect and heard my arrow hit in the brush beyond him. A clean pass through. He ran off a hundred yards, bedded down, and died right there. Right there in plain view. No tough trailing job. No drama. No heartbreak. Normally torture and suffering follow me around bowhunting elk like flies follow after maggots, but not today.

I looked down at the plaid pattern on the sleeve of my jacket. Magic. Pure and simple magic. While I was thus pondering the miracle of my birthday jacket my mind's eye hearkened back to the old days when a simple plaid shirt was all the man of bow and arrow needed, back to the days of Fred Bear, Howard Hill, and the Bee Gees. I thought of thumbing through my Dad's ancient "Archer's Bible" as a young boy and seeing pictures of those early archers in plain shirts and canvas pants and felt hats. I thought back to my days in junior high when I would get teased for being a dork and my mother would tell me that it is not what is on the outside but what is on the inside that matters. I was beginning to believe that this timeless advice is as true for bowhunters as it is for junior high dorks.

Besides the two nice caribou bulls and the six point bull elk, by the end of September I had also killed a huge whitetail buck that grossed 174 inches out of wobbly eight foot ladder stand attached to a scrubby little juniper tree, a couple whitetail does, and my first ever archery antelope buck out of a ground blind. Some were taken on private land, some on public land, but all with archery equipment. All completely fair chase, and all while wearing the green plaid jacket.

By season's end in 2007 I would add a couple more does, a wild buffalo near West Yellowstone, Montana and a javelina in Arizona. Regulations required that I shoot the buffalo with a rifle, although I could have easily shot the big bull with my bow. To be fair, I could have worn my Barney the Purple Dinosaur camo and killed the buffalo. Not exactly the wiliest of God's creations.

In 2008, I decided to take my new theme of hunt simplification to the next level. Before the season started, I emptied my daypack on the floor of my office. I was surprised how much that pile of junk looked like a Cabela's close-out bin. Only those items deemed absolutely necessary went back in. Now my daypack weighs about 8 pounds. With a lighter daypack and my trusty green plaid jacket, I had another great season. Not quite as spectacular as before, but by my standards pretty awesome nonetheless. I shot another six point bull out of the same ladder stand that I had killed the big whitetail out of the year before. I killed another antelope, a few whitetail does, and shot a little mule deer buck spot-and-stalk.

This past season, I determined that the next evolution in my quest was to go completely camo-free. The only camo I grandfathered in was on my bow, because I really like my bow. I needed was some camo free pants and a new daypack. This was way harder than I had first imagined. Just try to go out and buy a good hunting daypack and a sturdy pair of hunting pants that is not camo, and you'll see what I mean. In the end, I went to the place one would naturally turn when faced with a vexing personal fashion issue – The United States Government. After literally months of looking around, I finally found two pair of pants at Smith and Edwards Army Surplus Store in Utah, one pair olive green, the other dark brown. I also came up with a green canvas daypack, although at first glace you'd expect a pack like that to have a couple of textbooks called "The Criminalization of Capitalism", and "Global Warming - To Die For" inside and a pair of grimy open toed sandals tied to the top of it. An upgrade in this area is still on the front burner, but I was at long last ready for my truest test to go camo free.

And the results? I shot a Boone and Crockett sized black bear spot-and-stalk during the spring season, bow killed another huge whitetail that scores 153 by literally walking out and standing on a fallen tree to get closer to the deer crossing. By sheer luck I shot a Pope and Young six point bull elk one morning in the wide open by using the only cover I had, a fence brace. I got a decent antelope buck point-blank out of a treestand about 6 feet in the air. I bought a pocket full of extra doe tags and then attached each and every one to an archery killed doe. In fact, I completely tagged out, something I had never done before, not even once in my 25 years of hunting. All 100% legal and 100% camo free.

As usual, I found out my dear Mother was right. It is not what is on the outside but what is on the inside that counts. On the outside, camo-free plaid works for me. On the inside I suppose I've learned to be creative with whatever cover I have to work with, to keep the wind in my face at all costs, to simply sit still a little longer, and to be doggedly persistent. Buy less camo and buy more gas. Shop less, hunt more, that's what I say.

## BACKWARD IN TIME

*"Days should speak, and multitude of years should teach wisdom.*
*But there is a spirit in man: and the inspiration of the Almighty*
*giveth them understanding."*
*Job 32: 8-9*

High above the hay fields, I finally crest the tall ridge and wait for the earth to rotate another degree or two and give me shooting light. A trickle of sweat cools on my lower back so I pull off my pack, unroll my fleece jacket, and put my flashlight away. Already it's cloudy in the dark of morning and the gusty wind shudders the sagebrush and sways the tops of the big fir trees. It's going to be a blustery October day. It was cloudy last year too, but on that day there was no wind and the ground was damp from a light rain that had fallen in the night. Last year. What a great day that was!

I put my jacket on, drink some water, and slowly walk north across the sagebrush flat. I skirt the backside of a finger ridge, staying out of view of the canyon below. The wind is blowing sideways across my face, not perfect but not bad either. Gingerly, I sidehill the broad slope that drops into the broken canyon and set up next to a rock on a little point. It is still too dark to see well, but I sit down and start glassing anyway. The last few minutes before dawn are like watching a dim black and white movie, surreal and poetic but maddeningly difficult to enjoy. At least here I am out of the wind so I impatiently wait, watching the distant skylines take form.

When I can see enough to shoot, I shoulder my pack and angle farther across the hillside toward the timber. In childish anticipation, I break and fairly run to the last little rise and immediately glass the spot where my buck fell last year. I am probably within five feet of the spot from where I shot, and for a whole year the scene had played over and over in my mind. The familiar surroundings spark the memory and the powers of recollection spin time backward. Suddenly, once again, it was last year.

My brother-in-law Jason and I had hiked up in the dark the night before and dry-camped in a little grove of quakies. I killed a pine grouse on the way up and we roasted it and some canned stew over the coals of a small fire. We told hunting stories and talked of our lives under the stars, bothered only by the back and forth trampings of a fretful young moose, whose kitchen we had barged into uninvited. Two or three times a soft rain pattered the tarp over our bags, but we slept warm and dry.

Misty clouds obscured the coming of dawn, but we were up in time to grab a granola bar and go. Where the main ridge forked, Jason sent me right and he went left, a completely arbitrary decision he would later deeply regret.

The overcast extended the prime part of the morning, giving me more time to slowly pace across the open slope and glass. Not more than ten minutes after we separated, I caught the motion of a deer feeding along the edge of the timber below me. I nonchalantly raised my binoculars and literally gasped aloud when the magnified view registered. Thick, golden antlers branched impossibly wide and stretched skyward. I suddenly became aware of a hard pulse pounding in my neck and, at the same moment, my knees jellied. Feeding on a small cedar, very much undisturbed, was the most gigantic mule deer buck I had ever seen.

He was perhaps 200 yards below me in the draw, obscured by the brush so that the front third of him was all that I could see. Forcing myself to breathe over the growing knot of panic inside me, I eased into a sitting position for a better rest but then the curve of the hill covered up the deer completely. I slowly stood up again, wound the gun sling around my arm and riveted on the buck, centering in the scope the point where the neck and front shoulder join....

BOOM!

Silence. The quiet of a cloudy mountain dawn. A whisper of breeze against the sage. A jet arcing a white trail across the sky. I stood wobbly for several minutes, glued to the timber below and the open slope beyond. Nothing. I had seen nothing at the shot. No deer falling, no deer running, no deer anything. The shot felt good and I thought maybe I had heard the bullet hit with a crack, but then again maybe I hadn't. I had just shot at the biggest mule deer buck I had ever seen. Or had I? I began to experience the doubt all woodsmen know, like the fleeting glimpse of elk in the deadfall that, minutes later, you begin to wonder if you had really seen at all.

Finally, rubber-kneed and making all kinds of good behavior promises to Deity, I eased toward the spot. Moments later, a branch of antler above the sage and I knelt beside him. I was awestruck. Five on one side, four on the other. Bases as big as my wrist and a 32-inch spread. His gray and grizzled face supported his sturdy Roman nose, and he had half of one ear torn off from a fight. The back of his neck was black and blocky, even though it was a full month before the rut. This was quite simply a huge buck, and so swiftly did the .270 slug break his neck that green leaves still peppered his tongue.

I studied him for several minutes, overwhelmed by every angle. I got a soda from my pack and finally just sat down and looked at him, forever etching in my mind the marvelous scene I had just participated in. The mountain had graced me a tremendous gift, the rarity of which I knew full well. Everything was right. A gorgeous morning, a monster buck, a perfect shot. I drank it all in, completely fulfilled, until enough time passed that it seemed right to dress him out and go back for the horses.

A gust of wind brings me back to today. I lower my binoculars. Here, today, from this spot, there will be no monster buck. I am genuinely disappointed. For a full year I had harbored the irrational notion of standing again in this magical place and shooting another 30-incher. I knew better, I really did, but somehow the thought of it had been powerful enough to bring me back to the exact spot a year later. Maybe it was because of the place itself. I am standing where I stood a year ago, faced with the same vistas, circled by the same skylines. Somehow, just being here again makes last year seem more real, more complete.

As I glass the windy slopes, I'm reminded of a story told to me by the father of one of my hunting buddies. More than twenty years before, this man hiked into a dry bowl at the top of a bare, steep, and otherwise non-descript mountain and jumped three tremendous bucks. After that, year after year after year, he hiked into that bowl and never saw another antler. And yet, to this day, if you ask him where to find a big buck, he will instantly tell you about the three bucks in the bowl.

I stand there a few minutes, sunning in the warm memories of my buck. We are often drawn back to our places of good fortune, but we return to find that things are never the same. We're allowed a familiar peek at a day gone by, and then life goes on. Deep down, I knew I couldn't possibly ask for another 30-incher from this spot. Even with the special memories and great anticipation, the gusty wind is a constant reminder that this year is not last year, no matter how hard I try to make it so.

I drink a juice and zip up my pack. It was good to stand at this spot and remember that deer, but now it's time to move on. It is time to let last year's buck be last year's buck, and get going after this year's buck. I decide to cross the draw and work the ridge down to the south, hunting the bumps, and drop into the timber by mid-morning. I walk quickly, with a new resolve, and labor up the opposite hillside. Before I drop off the back side, I turn around and take a long look back.

Just in case.

*****

My partner Dave had made a crawling stalk and dropped a cow elk with one shot in a little stringer of pines. And I had killed a plump doe. Otherwise, it had been a long and exhausting hunt to return home so antlerless. Rounding the final corner before home, I was thinking of a hot shower and the chores I had to do before I could introduce the back of my head to a pillow. Turning into the driveway, the headlights swept across the yard and briefly illuminated a little green chair perched near the curb.

Instantly, I was transported backward in time to another yard and another chair. I saw eight-year-old me sitting mesmerized by the Saturday afternoon traffic, and listening for the rumble of the old Ford that would mean Dad had returned from deer hunting. I felt again the anticipation of seeing deer legs poking out of the box. I remembered the disappointment as the sun started to slip away, thinking that the Ford just *had* to be one of the next 10 cars to drive by. I heard again my mother hollering from the window for me to come in and go to bed, and remembered getting up off the chair, tense with frustration, and dragging my way back to the house.

I pulled into the driveway and shut off the truck. The number of lights glowing inside the house indicated that the little people were down but not out. Kim gave my odoriferous self a quick hug, and from downstairs a voice from the top bunk asked, "Dad did you get one?"

"Yeah, I got a doe but no elk. I'll tell you about it tomorrow. Go to sleep, buddy."

Hanging the deer up in the garage, I thought of the chair. Again my eight-year-old self appeared in my mind, and I remembered watching my Dad hang and skin his deer. It was then that I first felt both sorrow and awe for the dead deer. Sorrow for the glazed eyes and protruding tongue, awe at the antlers and fur and muscle that meant wild things in magical places. I would circle the swinging deer carcass, touch the bullet holes in the ribs and smell the meat. After Dad cut off the lower legs, I'd take them out back by the garden and make tracks in the dirt, burning the shapes and forms of those tracks into my memory. I'd feel the hide hanging over the back fence and visualize myself in the stories Dad told. Now, quite unexpectedly, the time had come when my young son would do these things.

Seating our young family at Sunday dinner the next day I recounted the hunt in as much detail as I could muster. Wide, amazed eyes listened as I told of hiking up the mountain in the dark under the stars, of seeing elk but no legal bulls, of the muley buck that gave us the slip, of Dave getting his cow, and finally how it was that a doe came to be hanging in our garage.

It suddenly struck me that this, right here, is my hunting heritage. I was, at this very moment, passing it on to eager, hopeful kids just as my father had passed it on to me. By dragging that chair to the corner, my boy had reminded me that I had the power to fuel that fire or to douse it. Not just for him, but for all the kids. Only I could rightly tell them the story of that hunt. All of a sudden I could see that it was my duty to teach them the ways and set the example. Right over Sunday dinner, I had been handed the opportunity to mold the next generation of hunters.

I continued with my story, now mentioning the bad shot that I might have taken but passed up, that I had seen other hunters but did not disturb their hunt, and that I had packed out my trash.

"I didn't get that six-by-six bull this trip, but there are still two weeks left," I confidently concluded.

Fairly busting with exuberance my five-year-old son replied, "Yeah, next time you'll get a twenty-by-one hundred, won't ya Dad!"

I glanced a smile over to Kim who grinned back. Wow! A twenty-by-one hundred bull elk. Now that would be worth waiting on a chair to see.

*****

A furious February wind piles the snow against the front doorstep. I sit reclined inside the house by the woodstove, reading a magazine article about a man who triumphed over a whitewater river in a distant land. There were logistics troubles. There were

1

weather troubles. There were fears, injuries, and hunger. Several times he fleeted with death. Later, when the man found himself back in the 50-hours-a-week, fax-it-to-me-ASAP life of bustle and careers, he paused to reflect on the contrast and freely admitted that it was the fury of the Colca River that sustains him.

I fold the magazine over my finger and settle into my chair, shutting my eyes. A mild melancholy wafts over me. I know well the sustenance of which he speaks. Although I don't have a list of whitewater rivers to conquer, the hunting season past is long gone and the next one will be a long time coming. For me, February is sheer endurance.

As I navigate the concertina wires of daily living, I will often pause and escape back into those autumn days afield that are forever etched into my mind, and the sustenance of those golden days somehow gives adequate endurance for the time being. Or else I project forward, the anticipation of the next Big Adventure sustaining me in the meanwhile. I pity those who have no such passion and refuge, but like most good gifts this renewal can also ebb into frustration and pain. A February of speeding from commitment to commitment can make a frosty October morning alone on a timbered ridge seem very distant indeed. I have been able to endure the Februarys because I know that the sustaining Octobers will surely come, just like they did before. But I keep getting older, and life keeps speeding up, and the lists of things to do never stops growing, and it seems harder and harder not to let my Februarys swallow my Octobers whole.

I get up and walk into my office. I tear the pages of the story out of the magazine and staple them together. I go to a shelf in the closet and pull out a bulging folder labeled "Favorite Outdoor Stories" and put the story in the folder and the folder back on the shelf. I peek out the window at the snow blowing horizontally across the lawn, and truly hope it is possible to balance all the critical centers of my life. What I pray for is the wisdom of less February, and the courage of more October.


*****


Bathed in the first rays of opening-day sunlight, the elk in the stubble field across the canyon began to stand out like candles on a birthday cake. Twelve become eighteen, then thirty-five, and then finally sixty. A semi downshifted on the highway grade below us, moaning loudly in the crisp morning air, but Dad and I were the only ones who seemed to notice. I looked at the semi through my binoculars. It looked close enough to hit with a rock. I scanned back to the elk. None of them even lifted their heads. Drawn to the tender greens of fall wheat, the elk were obviously undisturbed by the chatter of the highway.

Quite by chance, we'd discovered this group of elk a few days before the season and weren't entirely surprised to find them here. Still, it felt a little strange to be hunting elk and glassing semi trucks at the same time. This was definitely not your basic Teddy Roosevelt elk hunt. No frosty, high-mountain meadow here. No romantic horseback ride in the dark, no timberline vistas, no wilderness wall tent at the edge of a trout creek. We were sitting on a low rock knob between two grain fields right off a main highway. It had taken us less than twenty minutes to hike from the pickup to the knob. From our pre-dawn perch, however, I counted nine sets of headlights bumping up the dirt road past the grain fields and into the high country. At least three other groups of hunters had also driven up there and set up camps the night before. So even though the road noise bothered us a little, at least we had the place to ourselves. Just us, and as it turned out, sixty head of elk.

A series of trails out in the grain field funneled into a little saddle directly below us. Impatient at the sight of so many elk, I whispered to Dad that we should just go and get them.

"Nope," Dad said. "If anything over there gets them moving, those elk will barrel over here and be right in our laps. Now quit panting like a dog and relax a little."

Within an hour, most of the elk had moseyed out of the grain field and bedded down in the brush on the opposite hillside. Then I spotted two orange dots appear on the ridge above the elk. I hissed at Dad and pointed. He stiffened slightly, brought his knees up, and wound his sling around his arm. The two hunters stared at us through their binoculars. We stared back. They were quite oblivious of the sixty head of elk two hundred yards below them in the brush, even though every single elk had stood out if its bed and was staring up the hill at the direction of the hunters, ears wide.

"Here we go!" I whispered to Dad.

My knees began to chatter a bit and I slid my rifle across my lap, keeping my face glued to the binoculars, waiting for that first cow to bolt in our direction.

The two hunters stood there a minute or two gawking at us, and then they casually meandered on up the ridge away from the elk and disappeared over the top. Within minutes the elk were bedded again.

A finer metaphor for life would be hard to find - looking in vain for success across the canyon when it is actually standing up looking at you, undetected, right under your nose. We laughed at the two fellows' misfortune. A hesitant, merciful sort of laugh, lest the hunting gods curse us as well.

By then my Type-A personality had seen enough. I gathered my stuff and dropped off into the trees, working my way in a large circle around the elk, hoping to squeeze them between me and Dad. I had just crossed the upper field out of view of the bedded herd when out of nowhere, and only seventy yards in front of me, another small group of elk popped up. Among them was a spike bull, a very legal spike bull. I hesitated, knowing that there were at least four mature bulls in the big group. While I was hesitating, my gun went off three times, all nice lung shots. My first bull elk.

We'd found a spot. A tradition was started. Every opening day after that found our group of family and closest friends scattered around various points in those low hills surrounding the grain fields. The Rock Point, The Burning Bush, Hell Hill, Mine Ridge, Chicken Creek. These were places we named and came to know well. We gradually learned where all the gates in the fences were, the days and times when the ranch owner moved his cattle, where the elk hung out in a dry year. When elk ran, we generally knew where they were heading. When guns sounded, we generally knew who was shooting.

We killed elk virtually every year somewhere around the ranch. Most were spikes or raghorns, and occasionally one of us would draw a cow tag. Dad killed a dandy five-point one year near the Burning Bush and a few years later shot a 300 class six-point over in the Big Basin. My brother killed his first elk here also, another spike. I literally got off a shot at that bull as it ran across the hill with my pants down around my ankles, nature's call having come at a very inopportune moment. My brother-in-law discovered an excellent mule deer canyon on the Forest Service ground above the ranch where I killed a Brutus 32-inch five-by-four that still hangs on my wall. For a few years we watched a couple goliath bull moose that hung around a wallow off a little sideways timbered draw. It was like paradise. After a few years, it seemed like we had hunted there forever and we simply never considered that it wouldn't last.

But this world we live on is not a static place. Tilting on its gentle axis, the earth rises the sun and sets it. The moon goes from full to dark, the seasons from winter to fall. The lives we live and the places we know change along with the ebbing tides and the weather patterns. So it was with the ranch.

The owners sold the Rock Point to a guy named Brown, who still gave permission to hunt but also graded in a road out to the point and put in a modular home. A neighboring ranch locked their gates and posted their place, effectively reducing the hunting area by a third. Predictably, other hunters began to hunt along with us in the grainfields. It's hard to consistently kill elk anywhere without drawing a crowd, but it's doubly hard when you are within a mile or two of a paved highway. With such easy access, the ranch soon became a circus. After picking up what must have seemed like the hundred-thousandth beer can and after actually having a steer shot by an archer, the owner began to charge a $100.00 gate fee, which we reluctantly paid.

One opening day, toward the end, two pickups pulled in and parked right on the road, hoping to catch the elk running across the grainfield once the shooting started. Besides our four hunters, there were seven others on the ridge along Garden Creek. Three guys and a four-wheeler were in the CRP on the adjoining ranch to the south. A plume of dust hung over the road most of the day from the constant stream of pickups and four-wheelers drifting in and out, looking for an easy elk.

A couple of days later Dad overheard a cashier at a gas station-convenience store giving some guy directions to the ranch, telling him that if he wanted to kill an elk all he had to do was pull in before daylight and wait for the elk to spill out across the fields. That was it. The proverbial final straw. After nine years, it was time to move on.

More than once, I had harbored the thought that one day I might sit on the Rock Point with my two sons and wait for the sun to rise on sixty head of elk and be the only ones who knew of it. But you can never plan for the sun to rise on elk. Never. That morning is long gone, tucked away in the safety deposit box of good memories, to be pulled out and shared on long road trips and around campfires and the like. In the end, we were plain lucky for all those times we had hunting elk by ourselves in those grain fields within sight of a major highway and that is all there is to it.

I'm sure people will still hunt elk in those grain fields. But for us, at least for now, there will have to be new elk and new places. We'll conjure up a new spot and a new tradition, just like we did before. Maybe we'll get nine good years out of that one before the wanderings of time and circumstance will send us up the trail again. Maybe I'll see my boys kill their first elk there. Maybe I'll shoot my first big six-point there. Who knows? Maybe even on our first morning there the sun will rise on sixty elk across the canyon.

But these are things that you can't plan for, much less expect. These are the unknowns of the gray morning dawns. Realistically, all you can do is get out there and hunt, enjoy it while you've got it, and know that sooner or later it will be time to move on.

*****

It's 1:30 in the morning and time to change music. The white lines on the southbound lane of I-15 blip through the headlights at staccato pace. I'm making good time since my driving shift started in Provo. I'd been listening to the rather eclectic *4-Non Blondes* on the headphones, but now I want something a little more mellow, and settle on *Smooth 70's*, one of those two CD sets advertised on TV and not found in stores. The night is bright under a January full moon, the passing valleys and mountains reflecting in remarkable detail. Especially the mountain ranges, the moon glow off the snow providing contrast reminiscent of an Ansell Adams photograph.

Everyone else is asleep. My hunting buddy John and my son Jacob are on the mattress wedged into the back of the Suburban. My wife Kim is curled up on the second seat, and my daughter Jessi is stretched out in the passenger seat. Our oldest two kids had to miss this trip, victimized by membership on their high school basketball teams. We're heading for Arizona, and the purpose of this trip depends on who you ask. Jacob and I are going down to archery hunt for javelina. Kim is going to visit her mother. John is hunting during the day and visiting relatives at night. Jessi is getting out of a week of school. In the process, all of us are getting out of the Montana winter to spend a week in Arizona. Temporarily turning our backs on our lives and getting out of town. Road-tripping. Wanderlusting. And I can never decide which I like better, the being there or the getting out.

The exits come and go, gradually spacing themselves farther apart as we drive south, the orange glow of the urban Wasatch front finally behind us. Through the music my mind wanders in incongruent circles, but I'm energized simply by the freedom of driving through the bright night and the anticipation of a few days of prowling around the Arizona desert. When I pass Scipio and its small smattering of night lights, I have an urge to pull over and spend some time. Scipio. Has a nice ring to it. I'd want to hike the cedar canyons to see if they hold any big muley bucks. Eat at the local diner. Meet the football coach. Find out who lives under that solitary yard light miles out in the valley, to see if I recognize in them the people I know who live in similar isolation in Montana. Talk with the locals and find out how they got here and what makes them stay. Get to know the secret fishing holes. Spend a few weeks. Connect with the place a little. But I have no connections here, and probably never will, and drive by at 85 miles an hour.

The late hour and the 70's music envelope me in nostalgia, and I feel a true sense of loss at the passing of Scipio. So many Scipios, so little time. So many adventures, such limited resources. So much freedom tethered to so many responsibilities. I make promises to myself to slow down a little, to wring more out of life, to get to know my own town the way I want to know Scipio. Promises which I know are easily made late at night, listening to old music, driving under a full moon, but much harder to remember when the sun rises and the day bustles to life and the infinite distractions of the modern world begin to cyclone overhead.

Still, I sometimes imagine gathering the family at the dinner table and announcing to them out of the blue that we are selling the house and the business and packing up and going someplace else. Someplace far away with good hunting. As their jaws drop, I ask for votes for either Alaska or New Zealand. Maybe even South Africa. Maybe eventually all three. Sometimes I think it would be a grand experience, romantic and liberating, an enlargement of the soul. Other times I think of the cabins.

Every so often while wandering around in the wilds of the West I come upon an old broken down log cabin. I usually poke around a little, looking for an overlooked antique or two, wondering who made it and why. And more importantly, why they left. Normally I figure the cabin was made by either mountain man or miner, and run off by bad luck or Indian arrows or the long winters or something of the like. Every so often, if the cabin is in a spot conducive to the thought and I take the time to immerse myself, it becomes more personal.

One cold September morning, after an early storm left a couple of inches of snow in the mountains, I had tramped around in the dark timber country west of Helena looking for a bull elk to shoot with my bow. About mid-day, I came off the top of a little bench and found a rotten old cabin tucked into the mouth of a tight little draw, a few yards above a little brook. Admiring the setting, a line from the movie *Jeremiah Johnson* popped into my head. "Mountains in back. Water in front. Very little wind. This will be a good place to live." I scratched around a bit and decided to eat my lunch here, so I pulled off my daypack, brushed the snow off of a fallen log, and got a sandwich out.

I relaxed as I ate, my mind wandering, and glancing at the cabin suddenly imagined in my mind one of my square-jawed Scandinavian ancestors coming West, full of big hopes and bigger dreams, and the ageless family wanderlust coursing thick through his veins. I visualized him standing over a fallen lodgepole just up the hill, broad-shouldered and lean, expertly knocking out a notch with a double-bitted ax, building with his calloused hands his very own gold mine or big cattle ranch. I imagined a blue-eyed woman alongside, resilient and strong, puffing wisps of her long, sandy hair out of her face while she sets the notched log. I thought that they would surely toil all day, building the cabin row by slow row, and at night they would talk of their achievements sparingly and their fears not at all. I thought of her standing back while he finally hangs the split lumber door, the cabin now complete. Bent over the bottom hinge, he glances back at her and smiles through the two square-headed nails he holds in the corner of his mouth. She brushes her hair behind her ear with her hand, smiles back, and pats her palms together.

Now the split lumber door lies moldering and broken amongst a litter of rusted iron parts. The roof caved in years ago, the walls half-sunken over time. Out of the pine duff I kick up an old tin can, rusted chocolate. Why can I never bring myself to think this story has a happy ending? And why this persistent fear that whispers that this broken down cabin is the consequence of dreaming without planning, of wanderlust without prudence? Regardless, the weather-beaten log remains leave a sense of harsh reality, the long and brutal Montana winters this high in the mountains just as capable of breaking down the people as the old wooden cabin.

So I temper my desire to simply ride off into the sunset with a degree of caution, although I reserve the right to revisit the issue once the kids are grown. In the meantime, I'll have to be content to drive out of the Montana winter for a week of archery hunting for javelina in Arizona. It'll be a nice break, but not nearly enough time to really connect. Then we'll come home. As soon as I get back, I'll do my best to clear off my desk and get ready to head over to Idaho for a weekend or two of steelhead fishing. When I get back from that, I'll apply for a deer tag in Wyoming or plan a fishing trip to Alaska or maybe a cruise to Mexico with Kim. After that, maybe a turkey hunt in eastern Montana or a few afternoons looking for a spring bear. Maybe someday I'll even get to New Zealand for a red stag. And then I'll come home again.

By now I am passing the town of Beaver, and I'm curious why a town the size of a Boy Scout Jamboree needs two exits. I rummage around the seats looking for a snack to keep me awake.

Cedar City seems like a long time coming and when it does I am really tired, the drive through the night wearing me down. Forty-five minutes later when I get to St. George, I have absolutely no desire to pull over for a few days and connect. I just want to get some sleep. I exit the freeway at a truck stop on the south end of St. George and Kim wakes up when I start the gas pump. That's good. It's her turn to drive anyway. Before the tank fills everyone is up and inside the convenience store, bleary-eyed, aimlessly rooting around in their socks, waiting for their turn at the bathroom. John and Jacob are pumping quarters into a crane game trying to win a small teddy bear or a cheap watch, unconcerned about their comical blanket hair.

Kim asks for directions as I pull the sleeping bag over me. Hopefully she can make it to Vegas, maybe even to Kingman. It's only another three hours from Kingman.

# GROWLY OLD BULL

*"Ask, and it shall be given you; seek, and ye shall find;knock, and it shall be opened unto you: For every one that asketh receiveth; and he that seeketh findeth" Matthew 7:7-8*

Powdery dust puffs from my boots as I march up the old cow trail toward my pickup. It's hot. August hot. More bad luck, this weather. I take off my camo cap, a blackish ring of sweat bleeding out toward the brim, and wipe my face with my forearm. I look out across the miles and miles of timber, which only magnifies the folly of my pursuit. How impossible, in all these mountains, in all this crunchy, dry country, to find that one growly old bull. Especially in this heat. Especially this year, with such limited time to hunt. This autumn caught me and my wife Kim smack in the middle of building a house, and a month before the season our very first employee had quit our small business and hired on with a competitor. Such good luck to draw this highly coveted tag. Such bad luck swirling all around it.

I start up the trail again, drips of facial sweat pocking the dust. Day three, in the books. Three out of the fifteen allowed for the limited entry, either sex elk permit folded neatly in my wallet. Even though it reads "either sex", my tag is really permission to hunt the big, mature bulls that are otherwise protected in this carefully managed area near Island Park, Idaho. Pleased most years to shoot a cow or a spike, I had applied hopelessly for this permit year after year looking for my ticket to a real wall-hanger. Back in July, when the cartoon hunter on the Idaho Fish and Game's website did the happy dance before my disbelieving eyes, I finally had it. This tag would be marked "For Brutus Bull Only". It was, therefore, especially tantalizing when a hoarse, growly bugle had foghorned from the timber in the pre-dawn gloom of opening morning. A mature, herd-bull bugle that quit even before the orange glow of daybreak had erased all the stars. Three hard days of hunting later and I still hadn't even seen him, but I'm guessing that he must be a huge six-by-six, or maybe even a monster seven. Precisely the type of bull worthy of my tag.

Fifteen minutes later I reach the pickup. I kick the rock where I hid my keys and open the cab, hot air gushing out when the door opens. Due to the unusual interferences, I optimistically conjured up a grand plan for this hunt. My lifelong friend Scott would scout the area during archery season, since he lives nearby and I am a six hour drive away. He would certainly have the scoop on a big bull or two by the end of archery season and just in time for my rifle hunt. I would drive down the day before the opener, have Scott show me the worthy bull and then, the next morning, have him take my smiling picture behind its huge rack. Then I could get home and give some attention to all the other chaos. I knew better than to put such a snug little calendar together for an elk hunt, but at the time it seemed like the only way to make it work. Even as Scott's reports of hot, dismal conditions and very few elk sightings continued through September, I kept the faith. Sooner or later, the weather, and my luck, had to change.

Now three days into my hunt, and the keepers of the mountains had rather ruthlessly trashed my tidy little plan. Gritting my teeth against the now-likely prospect of failure and the thought of the stacks that would assuredly be piled on my desk at home, I start the truck and drive away.

At home I had hoped to clear both my head and my desk. I managed neither. I had tried for ten years to draw this tag and now I had it. Kim and I had scrimped and saved, fixed and painted, bought and sold for fifteen years to get to build a house and now we were building it. Both at the same time. And then, like the knockout left hook that follows a sharp jab, there was the debacle at work that all by itself could have consumed a month or two. It was as if both sides of the scale sagged clear to the ground. There was no possibility of balance. Only gravity. I was flat-out exhausted, physically and mentally. And, relentlessly, the clock ticked and the desk overflowed.

A week later, I was at the construction site of our new home. I caught Troy, our contractor, on his way out and we chatted about the comings and goings of the house. He left for the day and I went in to see what had been done. Sawdust particles sparkled in the shafts of light coming through the upstairs windows. It smelled like glue and new plywood and power tools. It was quiet and I was alone. For a moment I stood where the living room would be and looked at the bare studs that would become the fireplace. Breathing deeply, I imagined the growly old bull and just how good he would look mounted there. Right then, I had a moment of clarity. What could I possibly be thinking? The house was going to get built. The business would stay afloat. I had less than a week to go on a hunt that I had tried for ten years to draw and I was going to miss it because I wanted to be sure the plumber got there on Wednesday? Or because of some hassle at work that I, ultimately, had no control over? Stuff that, ten years from now, I wouldn't even remember? For these things I would leave the mountains and the growly old bull? For a plumber? I hurried home. I needed to get packed.

I told Kim that evening that I was either going to notch that elk tag or burn it, but either way I was going to quit crying about the hot weather and drive down there and get that growly old bull fair and square. It was time to quit wondering if he was worthy of me and start to show that I was worthy of him. I packed with resolve, and slept that night the best I had in weeks. I was still plumb exhausted, but I was focused. Early the next morning, I unplugged the cell phone and drove away.

Scott skipped work that first morning to join me. It had been hot every day since I left and the immediate forecast called for more of the same. Getting out of the truck in the morning darkness it was clear and very warm as usual, but when we dropped into the timber we walked into a dense fog. Just my luck. But the fog kept the growly old bull bugling and we set up above him, certain we were in the right spot but unable to see more than a few yards. The bull bugled again, lower on the hill. We moved down a little ways and set up again. Another growly bugle, again down the ridge. We grinned at each other like a pair of wolves. Of course. The hot summer must have changed their feeding habits and the elk had reversed their pattern. Instead of feeding down on the flats and bedding in the timber, these elk were feeding in the upper parks and bedding lower on slopes, nearer the cool, brushy creek bottoms. We backed out, not wanting to disturb the elk, and went looking for evidence. The tracks in the powdery trails were hard to read for sure, but we believed in our new theory. Scott had to work the next day, so I would be on my own.

At 3:30 the next morning I forced my spirit back into my body and somehow got out of bed. I needed to get well below the elk before daylight. I had never been so tired in my whole life. Strange, internal electrical jerks twitched my arms as I drove up the powdery mountain road. The fleeting shadows from the trees in the headlights startled me more than once, my mind unable to process quickly enough the information that they weren't moose or monsters or sasquatches. Once on top, I rolled the window down to listen for a bugle. My head bobbed like one of those dashboard dogs and I was afraid that I'd fall asleep and miss the whole morning. Somehow I steeled myself. I got my pack and gun and followed the old cow trail way down the canyon in the dark. Twice elk crashed away in the timber above me. I hoped desperately that the old bull was not among them. About three miles down the canyon I turned up, climbed to the ridge, and waited. I hadn't heard the bull bugle yet, and it was past the time that I normally had. I stood and waited for it to get light, afraid to even sit down. Finally from out of the warm gloom, I heard what sounded like the trailing of a bugle far above me. A few minutes later I heard it again, closer this time, sure it was a bugle but also unsure of where it was coming from. It sounded like it might be coming from the next canyon over. Ten minutes later another bugle, this time for sure the growly old bull and for sure in the next canyon. I piled off the hill, crossed the bottom, and carefully worked my way up a little finger toward the other ridge. In the dim black-and-white of pre-dawn, I heard an elk, or something, crackling through the brush above me, so I held still for several minutes. I would not blow this hunt. I absolutely would not blow this hunt! Once the unseen elk moved over the top, I Daniel Booned my way up through the brittle brush, alarmed at the noise I was making, and finally crawled over the crest of the ridge and peeked over the other side.

The first thing I saw was the top of a smallish four-point elk rack swing around and face me from about forty yards away. A second later I saw the ears of a cow radar me. The horrible implication of what I was seeing quickly registered.

No! Not after all of this! The growly old bull, a wimpish raghorn!? My guts braided up in a knot. The cow barked and both elk wheeled out of sight. I heard the wild crashing of many elk hooves clattering down the mountain and a thick cloud of dust trailed the elk down the mountainside. I ran over the top with my rifle ready and plopped down in an open chute. By then the raghorn and six or seven cows were moving single file through the trees on the opposite hill. I found him in the scope, but hesitated momentarily. Thank the Lord, because in the moment of that hesitation a growly old bugle blasted from the dark bottom of the canyon. Whew! For the second time that morning, my spirit returned to my body. More elk filtered up through the timber across the canyon, maybe 250 yards away. Cow, cow, spike, calf, cow. His girls were getting away. I readied myself. As if by magic there he was, flitting through the trees, his creamy body standing out, his thick horns sweeping way back, tines long and polished. Whoa! Big Bull! Forcing myself not to look at the horns, I centered him in the scope and fired. He dropped and thrashed into a little stand of Christmas trees out of sight. I chambered another shell and stayed riveted on the place. Elk were crashing off everywhere, but I would not lose this bull. I absolutely would not lose this bull!

After things had quieted down, I carefully stood up and moved to my left a few steps. Forty yards later I picked out a spot of blonde in the Christmas trees. I looked at it through the scope until my eyes watered. It was him. Was he up or down? I couldn't tell for sure. Moving further to the left, the angle improved and I could see the big bull piled up. It was plain that he was done. The growly old bull was dead.

I had applied for him for ten years and had planned for him for several months and had hunted for him for five solid days and had seen him alive for perhaps five seconds. He had taken me to the physical and emotional brink. And now there he was, lying across the canyon in a patch of Christmas trees. As if walking out from under a huge weight, I made my way across the canyon and over to him, taking a moment on bended knee to sincerely thank God, the Maker of all elk.

Just like that, and my luck had changed. He is an awesome six-by-six with sweeping, beautiful antlers and tremendous daggers. The main beams are over 50 inches, and his mass and character are superb. I especially like his character. Hefting his tremendous rack I was, and still am, completely satisfied that my tidy little plan failed and that I didn't just drive up and kill him on opening day. I'm proud that he took me to the point of strange little electrical jerks in my arms. I'm not ashamed in any way that the pursuit of him made the fleeting shadows of the headlights look like moose or monsters or sasquatches. I'm honored that my head bobbed like a dashboard dog for him. He is worthy of all of it.

Just as I supposed, the house did indeed get built. In fact, I kind of stayed out of it after a while and let the people who build houses do their thing. It turned out great. The competent people around me at work excelled and the business not only survived but has thrived. I think of the profound implications of these things when I remember the growly old bull. I ponder the delicate connection between willpower and circumstance in what we call luck. I think of timing and balance, fortitude and grace. I'm reminded of these things often, since I see him almost every day. He is very stately over the new fireplace.

## THE SACRIFICIAL RAM

*"Behold, to obey is better than sacrifice,*
*and to hearken than the fat of rams".*
*1 Samuel 15:22*

So, how long are we just gonna sit here?" Jake whispered sideways in my ear.

"Until dark if we have to," I whispered back. "Relax a little."

We flattened against the top of a cone-shaped clay knob and peeked over. Propping out my binoculars, I counted through the heat waves again. Eleven. Eleven bighorn rams, about half of them on their feet milling around. I focused on the big boy. He was bedded about halfway down the slope with two other rams. My rangefinder showed 158 yards. The closest ram was 120. Still too far, but we were right where three little draws funneled together and the wind was good. Yes, we would wait here until dark if we had to.

It took a series of miracles for us to even be here, out in the Missouri River Breaks of Montana bow-hunting bighorn sheep. Not your average, garden variety miracles either, but actual water-to-wine, nets-full-of-fishes, Lazarus-come-forth type of miracles. Jake had just graduated from high school and was planning for his missionary service by late summer, which meant he would miss the next two hunting seasons. Since he wanted to keep building bonus points while he was away and since you couldn't just apply for points in Montana at the time, we had scoured the regulations and put Jake in for hunts with the longest possible drawing odds precisely so he wouldn't draw. The choice for bighorn sheep was easy, despite the fact that we live a scant half an hour drive from the famed lower Rock Creek unit. When we sat at the computer and typed in "680-00" on Jake's sheep application, I knew that the year before 3,633 first choice applicants had applied for only 20 tags.

As bad luck would have it, the very morning after Jake had completed his last interview and submitted the paperwork for his mission, a friend called and told me that the drawings for moose, sheep, and goat were on the internet. I ran upstairs and typed in my information. Nothing. I tried my wife and daughter. Zip. Almost as a second thought, I plugged in Jake's info and hit submit. My blood went cold when the screen said "Successful Sheep".

*"No, no, no, no,"* I chanted frantically as I actually closed down the computer and re-typed Jake's information. *"No, no, no…."*

As I chanted, I did the math in my head. It was now the third week in June. It usually takes about three weeks to get a mission call back and then usually another four to six weeks before you report to the Missionary Training Center. None of this even came close to adding up to the 15th of September. I finished typing and hit "submit" again. It said "Successful Sheep" again. *Oh no!*

I debated whether or not I should even tell Jake, but when he got home from work that day all I could do was show him the computer screen and say, "Have faith. You'll have to have faith."

His face lit up when it registered what "Successful Sheep" meant, and then dulled slightly when it registered what "have faith" meant. Jake simply walked to his room and grabbed his bow, went outside, and started shooting.

The next Sunday at church Jake handed me his Bible, opened to Genesis Chapter 22, and whispered for me to read verse 13. "And Abraham lifted up his eyes, and looked, and behold behind him a ram caught in a thicket by his horns: and Abraham went and took the ram, and offered him up for a burnt offering in the stead of his son."

"Get it?" Jake said. "I'm supposed to go offer a ram as a sacrifice before my mission."

"Yeah," I said. "The sacrificial ram. And we should make sure to get a first-born male without blemish, preferably one scoring at least 190 Boone and Crockett points."

After a divinely inspired delay by our local leader in submitting his portion of the paperwork, the envelope with Jake's mission call arrived in the mail. He could be spending the next two years almost anywhere in the world, and yet I was all a-twitter about when, not where. He opened it up and started to read. He would serve in Phoenix, Arizona. So far, so good. I braced myself for the next sentence, and I was sure I heard harps and cherubic choirs of angels singing Hallelujah above me when Jake read that he was to report October 1.

In the meantime, we had learned of another miracle. For the first time ever, an early archery-only season for sheep tag holders would open September 5th until the 14th. By the power and grace of the Montana Fish, Wildlife, and Parks we now had ten extra days of hunting. It was time to go to work.

We talked to former tag holders, landowners, and taxidermists. I contacted a game warden from Havre named Shane Reno who was so helpful that I offered him a job in customer service in my business. We bought all kinds of maps, sheep videos, and sheep hunting books. I thought Jake was going to wear out his bow shooting the 3-D deer target in our yard that now sported enormous cardboard sheep horns. We went on a three day scouting trip. Anything we did together revolved around the sacrificial ram.

One evening we were in a restaurant sizing up a sheep mount. "Pretty heavy at the base. A softball-sized hole, but it tapers out fast and has a pretty weak jaw drop. Decent curl, but maybe a little tight." Our waitress rolled her eyes. "Oh," Jake said. "Not you. The ram."

The day finally came when we drove two time zones past the middle of nowhere and creaked the door open to a BLM cabin, ditching our stuff to get in an hour of glassing before dark. We located 8 rams that evening, including one about three miles away that looked like an absolute giant. The next morning none of the rams we had put to bed could be found, so we took off in the direction of the big ram. We parked the quads and started hoofing it up a wash to get to the top of a brutal looking rim. On the way in we bumped eight or nine rams feeding in the bottom, but they were mostly small and ran off through the sagebrush before we could really look them over. We stayed on course and scrabbled up to the top of the cliff. We found a few more decent rams but could not locate the big boy. However, from up on top we re-located the rams we had bumped in the morning.

I dialed up the spotting scope, checking out the rams while Jake was putting a lizard he had caught into an empty water bottle.

"Hey, Jake," I said. "Come check out this one."

Jake squinted into the scope. His eyebrows shot up and that's when he started panting like a dog. "I likey that one!"

"Are you absolutely sure. You may never, ever do this again. Would you be once-in-a-lifetime thrilled to kill that ram with your bow?"

"Oh, yeah!"

By now it was about 80 degrees and we had to find a way off the rim, across the wash, up to the top of the next rim, and then locate the rams somewhere in a series of small but very steep clay draws. We memorized a few landmarks and took off. Hiking in the Missouri River Breaks is like standing on one foot to tie your shoes, it's a lot harder than it looks. At one point we had to slide off a crumbly little cliff maybe ten feet tall, straddle a few boulders to get into the bottom, and then crawl through a four foot tunnel carved out by the wash. I kept wondering who was going to be sacrificed first, me or the ram.

A couple hours later we crept over a second little ridge. The rams were not in the first draw as we had expected, but we knew we had to be close. I put the spotting scope down and started to glass with my binoculars. Jake was glassing to my left. All at once I saw ram horns appear over the sagebrush a couple hundred yards directly below me.

I ducked behind a knob of crumbly clay that looked like an African termite mound and clicked my fingers to get Jake's attention. He peeked over his shoulder and froze. He slowly squatted down and crawled on all fours beside me. I waited a few minutes and bellied up to the top of the knob. I found eleven rams total, but the first one still stood at full alert, staring us down. The other rams were feeding along, unconcerned, and after about 45 minutes the first ram finally moved up to the others and bedded down. Jake impatiently wanted to make a move, but I told him we'd wait. Wait until dark if we had to. He looked the situation over for himself, and reluctantly agreed that there was not much doing right then. So we waited. And waited. Three long, hot hours we waited.

Finally, the rams all got up, stretched, and milled around for a few minutes. To our horror, they started angling directly away from us but toward the ridge to our left. I told Jake that if he wanted to chance making a move, it was now or never. I would stay on the knob and direct him with hand signals. He gathered up his bow, checked his release, and grinned at me like a hungry wolf.

Thirty yards of open flat lay between the clay cone and the ridgeline. Jake slithered across the opening on his belly and dropped into the opposite draw undetected. Whew. That was the hard part, or so I thought.

He looked at me through his binoculars and I waved him further down the draw. He took like three steps and looked again. I waved him down again. He took two more steps and looked again. I then directed an intricate but simplified series of hand signals that any person of ordinary intelligence could have easily understood as meaning, "go forty yards farther down the draw, ease up to the ridge, come to full draw and shoot the largest ram, which will be slightly to your right and third in line."

For some reason, intelligence deficit most likely, Jake just wasn't getting it and the rams were getting closer. I finally just waved him toward the ridge. The rams were now in two groups. There were eight smaller rams in a bunch which would be directly below Jake, and the big one was in a group of three slightly to the right, just as my obvious hand signals had indicated.

At this point the DVR in my mind hits "record", and I will forever see Jake kneeling just below the ridge opposite the sheep, coming to full draw, and easing toward the rams not more than 30 yards away. All eleven ram heads suddenly yank up and stare, while he momentarily points his drawn bow at the group of eight small rams. I begin to panic but then he swings his bow to the right and, as I focus my binoculars on the big ram, I hear his bow shoot. Never to be erased is the sight of those eleven rams blowing off down the hill and balling up on a little ledge, changing directions in the process. The big ram turns, blood pouring perfect from behind the front shoulder. *"Holy shnikes! Jake just smoked that huge ram!"* The old ram pauses and stumbles and the other sheep run away. He then flips over and tumbles wildly in a dozen airborne somersaults while Jake is up on the ridge doing the Abrahamic happy dance. It all seems, well, downright miraculous.

We fairly float off the hill and approach the ram. He is big and he is beautiful. His horns measure 42 and 38 inches, and we age him at 7 ½ years old. His bases are a decent 15 inches and he carries his mass extremely well. The back side of one horn is notched and jagged from banging heads with other rams, but that only adds to his character. Jake is jabbering around with a big old sacrificial ram smile plastered on his face. We take a bunch of pictures, green score him at an amazing 186, cape and quarter him, and by late evening we have the ram packed out and hanging from the meat pole, along with a pack rat and a four foot rattlesnake. Another great day in the Breaks.

Three weeks later Kim and I dropped Jake off to start his two years of missionary service, all shined up in a new suit and tie. Even as his Mom was bawling her eyes out, Jake still had that big old smile plastered on his face. Choking up a bit myself, I told him that no matter what comes his way he should always work hard, be obedient, and keep the faith. I reminded him to do his duty, keep on smiling, and when things get tough he should just remember that the Lord had already pre-blessed him mightily for his service with the sacrificial ram.

Reflecting on those words, I suppose what I meant was to freely believe in miracles, always find a way to have a little more faith, and if you ever get a chance at a sacrificial ram you really must try the Missouri River Breaks in Montana.

## HOLLY'S COW

*"Out of the mouth of babes and sucklings*
*hast thou ordained strength" Psalms 8:2*

I gathered myself for a moment, my breath billowing in the frigid air. I eased my binoculars up and peeked over the ridge. Oh, yeah. Against the snowy landscape the elk looked like candy corns on a paper plate. I knew they had to be in here somewhere. One of William's workers had spotted them crossing over not more than three hours ago, and we hadn't found any fresh tracks indicating that they had moved out. William's ranch is situated in the barren steppe between the steep timber of the Pintler Mountains and the river bottoms of the Clark Fork, at first glance an unlikely looking place to find an elk. Several freezers full of elk meat over the years have proved that looks aren't everything, but the hunting is feast or famine since the elk are transients, pausing here temporarily on their way to somewhere else. I had anticipated finding them in the big, rocky basin where they normally hole up, but instead had to spend an extra hour hiking around in the five degree air to finally find them in this unlikely place. Right in the bottom of a skinny ravine, bedded in the wide open. Now we didn't have much time. I lowered my binoculars and slid off the ridge top and back to the group.

"About twenty head, bedded right in the bottom, south of the big draw."

"Any bulls?" my fourteen year old son Devin asked.

"No legal bulls that I could see, and I think I saw them all."

Devin made no attempt to disguise his disappointment. His elk permit only allowed for the taking of a brow-tined bull, which can be difficult to find this late in the season. William, our salt-of-the-earth neighbor who had called on the phone just as the kids bustled into the house after school, also had a bull permit. I had already tagged an elk. That left Holly, my twelve year old daughter. Little Holly was the proud owner of an antlerless elk permit. A cow tag.

Holly stood tentatively behind Devin and William, dressed in over-sized green Army-surplus wool pants that tucked into her snow pacs. I knew she had both long johns and Levi's on underneath. A hunter orange vest draped over her ski coat like a curtain, and she wore mix-and-match gloves that she had hastily plucked from the hat-and-glove box in the mud room. Her Dr. Seuss style stocking cap was pulled tight to her eyebrows, her rosy cheeks complimenting her expressionless face. The Winchester youth model .243 seemed absurdly large slung over her little shoulders. She looked very small to kill an elk.

I took a quick inventory of the situation. From where I saw them, the distance to the elk stretched well over a quarter mile, too far for most accomplished hunters to shoot accurately, let alone a twelve year old girl with a small caliber rifle. The all-important wind was favorable, but we only had about twenty minutes before dark. We had to get closer. Somehow, we had to cross a hundred yards of bare ridge with no cover and in plain view of the elk without spooking them.

"What's your plan?" William asked.

"Well, we don't have time to circle all the way around before dark. How about I take Holly, since she has the cow tag, and try to cross over the draw and drop into the wash to get closer?"

William and his wife Margaret are old school Christian folk, and finer, more polite people would be hard to find. So he didn't come right out and call me an idiot, but his eyes told me that he didn't think there was any way I could get Holly across that open face without the elk ending up in the next county. I had to agree, but I would rather see the whole herd run away from a failed stalk than watch even one run off wounded because of an ill-advised long shot.

"Devin and I will go to the end of this draw below the elk in case they run out the bottom," William said, obviously assuming the elk were very soon to be up and running.

I gave them a few minutes to get below us and then turned to Holly. She looked at me expectantly. Unlike William, she believed. I took a minute and reached deep into my bag of hunting tricks, finally dusting off an idea that I'd heard about but never actually tried.

"Hand me your gun," I said. Without a word she unslung her rifle, careful that the barrel was pointed in a safe direction, and presented it to me. I checked the safety. It was on. I checked the chamber. No bullets.

"Good girl," I said, motioning to the gun. "Now, here's what we're going to do. If we just go traipsing over there those elk are out of here. So we need to look like something we're not. I'm going to carry the guns with the barrels forward and bend over at the waist. You grab my belt and put your head on the small of my back and we'll walk over there looking like a cow."

A silly smile arced over her face. "A moo cow?"

"Yep. A moo cow."

We practiced a few awkward steps before we swayed out of the draw and into view of the elk. So far, so good. About halfway across the open, every single elk stood up out of its bed and stared at us, ears flared wide. I just knew they were going to bolt, but they held their ground, seemingly mesmerized by the hunchbacked hunter-orange cow that kept giggling out the rear and growling shush-up out of the front.

Step by sway-backed step the curve of the ridge between the elk and us gradually covered the view of the elk's legs, then their bodies, and, impossibly, the last set of ears disappeared behind the snow. We hustled down to the bottom and belly crawled up to the ridge. I peeked over, still expecting to see elk rumps in the act of putting major distance between us. The elk had stayed put, but they were up and milling around, and one old cow had seen enough and was ambling toward the timber. We didn't have any time to lose. I stacked my daypack on a rock and Holly bellied into shooting position. She flattened in the snow, chambered a round, and looked through the scope.

"Which one?" she calmly asked, and right then I knew she was about to kill her first elk. I focused her on a cow that was separated slightly from the herd and gave her the green light. The gun cracked in the frigid air and I heard the *thwock* of a solid hit. The cow stayed up, hunched and splay-legged.

"Nice shot," I said, riveting my eyes on the elk through my binoculars. "Keep shooting until she's down."

I heard the bolt work evenly, then a slight pause, and the gun went off again. Another hit. Another shot, this time a miss. My insides were fluttering, still unfamiliar with my new role of guide and spectator, and I was glad I had both elbows planted in the snow to keep the binoculars steady. I glanced over at Holly and marvelled at how calmly she was about her business. I had seen grown men melt into a useless gob of nerves when it came time to shoot an elk. Buck fever. Many times I'd experienced it myself. Once I saw a man work the bolt action of his gun in a panic four times in a row, profaning that his gun was jammed, his cartridges falling harmlessly one by one to the dirt. Not my little Holly, at least not today. She smoothly chambered her last bullet, fired, and her cow went down.

We high-fived, and I circled my arms and squeezed past her coat until I felt her slender ribcage and gave Holly a big old bear hug. She wanted to hurry down there and see her elk, quite unaware of the extremely improbable luck we'd just had. We trotted up to her cow about the same time as William and Devin, and I had to try hard not to be smug. William gave me a glance.

"What? You never heard of the old bend-over-like-a-cow trick?" I teased.

"Oh, is that what that was?" William rolled his eyes slightly, but turned and gushed congratulations on Holly. Even Devin, normally tangled up in a big case of sibling rivalry, gave Holly her due.

By now the horizon had swallowed the sun in a kaleidoscope of pink and purple pastels, and sub-zero arctic air settled in and began to bite our faces. The elk died a short distance to a small road, and William offered to go for the truck. We rolled the elk over and I had Holly help clean and quarter the elk, saving out the liver for William. The warmth of where we bled and gutted the elk gave the sugary snow some pack, and as full darkness settled in my two oldest children spent the last daylight throwing bloody snowballs at each other.

This cow elk topped off the freezers for the year with a little to spare, but as I worked on skinning the elk quarters and dodging reddish snowballs, I knew the value in this short hunt isn't only in the packages of meat. It's out there somewhere in the process, in the place where I begin to see Holly not only as a quirky twelve year old girl, but as the capable young woman that can. Maybe for her it's in the moment when she can confidently look to her dad as the guy that might just have a trick or two up his sleeve when the odds look long. The real value comes when she begins to apply any one of the many object lessons of the hunt to her life, like learning to persistently look, despite the bitter cold and even in unlikely places, for whatever elusive joys in life she seeks. Or by learning that there really is a window of opportunity, that knowledge and effort are very often linked to timing in the thing we call luck. There is meaning in a hunt like this even for Devin, in learning that every day is not your day and being willing to sit back, watch, and cheer for your sister.

I took a moment from skinning to stand up and straighten my back. Devin and Holly were still chasing back and forth, laughing and carrying on as the entrail snowballs begin to have less and less and then, at last, no snow at all in them. They are just kids, too young and inexperienced to be able to give words to the seeds planted in their heads this day. But as the years go by, I hope to teach them that the wealth of these discoveries of the hunter can spill broad and deep, overflowing out of the mountains and becoming a permanent and vibrant part of the soul. They are, after all, lessons learned the hard way, by being out there and doing. The character of the hunt cannot be cheated in this. The more active and personal the participation, the closer to the bone, the richer the quietly whispered mysteries. Eventually this process matures and if enough time is taken to lie under the clouds or listen to the wind or watch an anthill or a herd of antelope or the stars, the questions begin to lead to deeper and more poignant questions, and a new layer of personal growth begins. This process is my heritage, my culture. It is my method of feeding both body and spirit. It is all tangled up in the person I am.

William's diesel pickup truck clattered up and we lugged the elk quarters into the back, the hocks already frozen solid. Devin and Holly planted themselves in the cab, cupping their hands over the defrost vents and stomping their numb feet against the floorboards, happy for any kind of heat. I reminded them how truly blessed they are to live in a place where they can get home from school, go out and kill an elk, and be home by dinner time. They each thanked William for letting us hunt his ranch, a nice gesture that I reminded them about while he was gone for the truck.

At home, Devin and Holly dashed inside for a hot bath, piecing out the story to their mother and the younger two kids as the layers peeled off and the bathtubs filled. I hung and bagged the elk quarters in the garage and put the hide in my truck to be traded for a couple of pairs of leather gloves at Pacific Hide in Missoula. When I finally made it inside and began to unlace my boots for the evening, Holly approached down the hall.

"Thanks for taking me," she smiled. "That was funny, being a cow."

"It's a good trick," I said "You did great." Just that fast the moment was over, somehow incomplete.

She turned away in her pink flannel jammies and disappeared back down the hall, punching the phone number of a friend into the cordless phone, looking small again.

# STREAKIN'

*"But call to remembrance the former days, in which,after ye were illuminated, ye endured a great fight of afflictions."*
*Hebrews 10:32*

Ten seconds after I shut the door to my pickup an elk bugled from across the river. Grabbing my bow, I puffed a breath straight into the frosty October air and a gentle southwest breeze carried it away. I shouldered my pack and wished myself good luck.

It had taken the better part of yesterday to set this whole thing up. Some elk had started hitting these hay fields at night, but they were leaving at the crack of dawn for the safety of a posted neighboring ranch. I also knew that it was almost impossible to get ahead of the elk from the fields without spooking them, so I decided to try to find a way in from the other side of the river. It was late evening before I got permission from the landowners, deciphered a way to wade across the river, and got my tree stand hung. I went to bed that night all a-flutter about my chances. Even though Montana's archery season was very nearly over I had a good feeling. This would be it. This had to be it. The streak would continue due to this little piece of bow-hunting brilliance.

A pencil line of orange pastel painted the eastern skyline as I made my way to the stand. Without warning an unseen branch caught my toe and pitched me forward. The bad news was that I was thigh-deep in the middle of the Clark Fork River when this happened. I held my bow above the water with one arm and doggy-paddled with the other, gasping for air as icy water lapped around my neck. My feet finally got under me and I waddled to the far bank, the dripping water melting the frost off the grass in a growing black circle. I pulled off one of my hip-boots and turned it upside down. A gallon of water gushed out, and for the first time I surrendered to the thought that maybe killing a bull elk with my bow just wasn't going to happen this year. That the streak might be coming to an inglorious end, right here on the banks of the Clark Fork River, shivering, soaking wet, dumping ice water out of my hip-boots. Gnashing my teeth, I looked up into the early morning heavens and said simply, "Why?"

But, partly at least, I knew why. There is a theory among the more superstitious of us hunters that if it is your day to kill then no matter how ill-prepared or late or stupid you are, you will kill. On the other hand, if it is not your day, then it doesn't matter one whit how early you get up or how hard you try or how well you hunt, you will not kill. The powers that referee whether or not it is your day are loosely categorized as "the hunting gods". It has always been curious to me that the hunting gods are mentioned in the plural, when in most instances it is in poor taste, if not a direct violation of the First Commandment, to profess more than one God. In the case of the hunting gods, I like to think of them as a whole committee of gods, lower case "g" gods, hunters who have passed on and who know first hand how to royally screw up a hunt, and whose post-mortal work is to get the lists of who will and who will not kill that day e-mailed to them from the desk of capital "G" God. As I shivered to pull my hip-boots back on and wade back to the truck, I got the distinct feeling that this was not going to be my day, or even more likely, my year. My mind reflected back to the transgression for which the hunting gods had evidently extended the long and merciless arm of justice.

Early in the season there had been one legitimate chance, one slam-dunk opportunity that evaded me mostly because I broke one of the other Ten Commandments, namely the one that says "Thou shalt not covet". That morning I had finally guessed right and the gray of not-quite-first-light found me directly above a pretty good herd of elk heading for the timber. They were all strung out coming up a little draw to a fence crossing, so I unrolled the 10 foot length of burlap that I had on my pack and hung it on the top wire of the fence. I checked to make sure I was downwind of the crossing and set up behind it. It's a pretty simple trick that works surprisingly well. The lead cow nosed up to the fence and I ranged her at 37 yards. Perfect. Right behind her was a nice, square 5-point bull. The cow hopped the fence and I drew my bow undetected. As the 5-point came up to the fence I saw out of the corner of my eye another bull, a dandy 6-point, coming up behind a few more cows. The 5-point jumped the fence and just stood there, broadside as big as day, a mere thirty-seven yards of still morning air between my drawn broadhead and his kill zone.

I hesitated.

Understand that I am not a hard-core trophy hunter when it comes to bull elk and bow-hunting, but I like big antlers as much as anybody and have been lucky to kill a few Pope and Young bulls with my bow. Mostly, though, I will shoot any legal, brow-tined bull that gives me a good opportunity. This was better than good. This was golden. A lay-up, and yet that big bull out of the corner of my eye held me at full draw. The 5-point trotted off. The big bull hung tight behind his cows which angled away. Finally, and with predictable results, I let my bow down. Even as the elk ran away, I knew I had blown it.

That night I sat in the hot tub on our back deck, looking into the stars, musing about the events of the morning. Repenting, basically. I played the scene over and over in my mind, fully regretting those few precious seconds of indecision. If I hadn't seen that big bull, the 5-point would be hanging in the meat cooler and we would be eating a celebration dinner in a restaurant. If only the big bull had just followed the others like he should have, he would be the one in the cooler and his cape would be at the taxidermist and I would mark a date on the calendar to get his antlers scored. It could have happened. I could have got away with it.

Yeah, right. I know full well the blizzard of things that can screw up a good opportunity, let alone to just to sit there at full draw while a better-than-legal bull elk parades broadside at 37 yards and you screw it up yourself. It wasn't like that bigger bull was going to get me on the cover of a magazine or anything like that, and that was a pretty decent five point that would have kept the streak going. The bottom line is there is no elk in the cooler, no cape at the taxidermist, and I'm going to eat warmed up leftovers instead of celebration prime rib. I deserve it. What an idiot!

One thing about it though, sooner or later that big bull will be back in there. I'll just have to keep after him...

My thoughts scrambled round and round like that for a while. Finally, I looked into the night sky and the stars that make the handle of the Big Dipper looked down on me in a cosmic frowny face. Yes, I had sinned. For the first time ever, I had not killed the gift bull when it was put in front of me, an elk I would have been perfectly happy with, simply for the coveting of 40 inches more antler. For that I was now truly sorry.

After that I buckled down and hunted hard, pushing a little extra. I tried new areas, followed up on tips from hunters and ranchers, hammered away on the areas I knew well. But the hunting gods were not in a forgiving mood just yet. Due to some unusual weather, the ranchers cut their hay late and changed the feeding patterns of the elk, the ever-evil wind goofed me up a few times, and sometimes the elk were just plain lucky. No matter what I did or where I went it always seemed like I was either a day early or two days late.

Before daylight one morning I heard a bull bugle, set up in front of him, and licked my chops when I heard him bugle again coming in perfect. He turned out to be a spike, not legal to shoot, and all by himself. When he got 80 yards out the wind shifted anyway and he blew out of there like his tail was on fire.

I got permission to sit in a tree-stand on my good friend Gene's ranch near Helmville where the sign looked like an elk avalanche had blown through. I saw nothing for the two days I had permission. The very next evening another guy took his choice of three bulls that hung around that very stand at close range like they had targets pinned to their chests. I braved the Blackfoot River bottom that was infested with grizzly bears, the jaws of my release tinking on the action of a 12 gauge shotgun loaded with slugs as I made my way in and out. Still no luck, but mama didn't raise no quitter so I kept going and going, even though by now the whole self-imposed ordeal was getting in my head big time and had kind of taken the fun out of it. One night I was sprawled out on my recliner, exhausted, watching a hunting show on TV where a guy put in a hard hunt and killed a big buck on the last hour of the last day and I caught myself mumbling, "oh please, oh please, oh please…"

Very near the end of the season I finally got the break I needed. Some elk began to hammer some hay fields which are almost impossible to approach from the ranch, but there had to be a way. I know the people who own the land on the other side of the river. Maybe if I could get permission from them I could figure out a way to get in front of the elk from that side, wade the river at a riffle, and set a stand on the other side at the bend. It would be perfect. Foolproof. What could go wrong?

Now that it's over, I can say that I had a streak of eight mature bull elk in a row with my bow. I suppose that's something to be proud of and grateful for, but when the sun went down that last evening and closed archery season, I was perfectly devastated. I pouted like a pathetic loser for a few days, stinging from my defeat and tormented by the nuisance memory of that 5-point bull broadside at 37 yards. After working through the five stages of grief, there was nothing else to do but start a new streak.

Hey, if I get a bull next year that would still be 9 out of 10. That is 90%, which is an A-minus, and I suppose I can be happy with being an A-minus bowhunter. Yes, I can like that. And come next fall, even if you are a brow-tined spike, it would be a very bad idea to hop the fence and just stand there.

# THE SCORPION FOSSIL

***"With the ancient is wisdom; and
in length of days understanding." Job 12:12***

A slender box comes out of the back seat of a pickup, the end flaps pulled away from the staples. A brand new PSE Scorpion slides out and Rob hands it to me. I hold the bow out in my left hand, balancing it in my wrist, sighting down the string, and my very first thought is, "Wow. It's a little bit heavy."

In every life there are unexpected moments of grace, little innocent events that only become meaningful by looking back on them. Like the moment I was at college, working on the grounds crew for spending money, shoveling up some mud by the campus library that had washed out of the flowers because of a broken sprinkler line. Two girls came out of the library together, a scatter-brained redhead named Janice and a good looking girl who I didn't know. She stood shyly back as Janice loudmouthed on and on, and right away I noticed how smoking hot this new girl looked in those little red jeans. If I could have known right then that this girl would become my wife, the mother of my four kids, and that we would spend a life of grand adventure together, well I probably would not have worn a ratty blue t-shirt that I stole from my roommate that said "Karl" on the back of it. In a similar way, if I could have seen right there in Gene's driveway the bowhunting nirvana that awaited me by way of that very PSE Scorpion, I would have gladly paid ten times the price.

Gene's good friend Rob is in the archery business and he was peddling some season-end bows at closeout discounts on a cash only basis. Rob assured me it was a great bargain, and a major upgrade from the bottom-of-the-line Browning I was currently shooting. I hefted the Scorpion again as he jabbered on about feet-per-second this and percentage-let-off that, noticing the single cam on bottom and large upper wheel, the vibration dampeners on the inside of the limbs, and the integrated 8 arrow quiver. Right away I liked how the grip fit my hand, and it seemed solid and sturdy. I pulled it back with my fingers. It drew back smooth and firm. I reached into my front pocket and peeled off three $100.00 bills into his out-stretched hand.

A few days later the bow is all decked out with a new rest and a new sight, and I am shooting it in the front yard. Rob was right about the bow being an upgrade. It shoots my heavy arrows snappy fast, groups the arrows well, and has a forgiving valley. I discover that my original concern about the weight of the bow is the best thing about it. The bow is heavy, but heavy in the way that a well balanced muzzleloader is heavy. Heavy but solid. I draw it back, anchor, and it settles in. For me, the really light bows always seem to wave about at full draw like a stiff summer wind is blowing. I practice all summer and feel pretty good when archery season arrives.

We get off to a great start by killing a wonderful 6 x 6 bull elk that grosses a hair over 320, at the time my best archery elk by a mile. I had been hunting this particular bull for a couple weeks but every devised strategy had thus far failed. About 5:30 one Monday afternoon we were 80 miles away from the elk in Alberton after watching our son Jake play in JV football game. I convinced Kim, which is of course the name of the girl in the smoking hot red jeans, to get a quick drive-through dinner instead of sitting down at a nice restaurant in Missoula. Then I sped like crazy to find out if I could get a line on where the bull was. When we got there a few cows were already feeding in the meadow. I parked a safe distance away and Kim stayed in the truck, curling up with a new magazine. I began stalking in, crawling the last 300 yards on hands and knees to a little waist high copse of dried grass on the edge of the meadow. By now it was almost dark and there were at least 50 head in the open. The big bull had just come out of the trees. He ran a smaller five-point bull out of the herd and began chasing and raking his cows around. Since all this action was taking place 200 yards away, my new PSE lay still in the grass. I decided to hold tight and take in the show for the last few minutes of light then slip back to the truck.

Suddenly, the big bull broke from the herd and trotted past me at 80 yards. I peeked up and saw a cow in the other end of the meadow. He bugled and chased at her, trying to get her over to the rest of the elk. I slid my hand through the wrist strap and gripped my new bow. A few seconds later he trotted behind the cow at 70 yards. I squeaked out a spikish little squeal on my bugle, then dropped the bugle in the grass and hooked my release to the string loop. Unbelievably, the bull wheeled in my direction and galloped over, slowing to a trot at just over 15 yards. Wide-eyed, I knelt up and drew back all in the same motion. The elk flared, but stopped broadside at 25 yards for just a second. The new bow swiftly settled and the arrow flew. *Crack!*

Now elk were running everywhere and a calf just about jumped over me in the hasty retreat. The bull disappeared over a rise, and I just sat still until everything was quiet again. By now it was plumb dark. With my trembling flashlight, I found my arrow covered with blood but despite twenty minutes of quiet looking I simply could not locate a blood trail. Since it was cool and I was not sure exactly where my arrow hit, and owing to the lack of a blood trail, I made the agonizing decision to come back in the morning.

But there was no drama. Right at daylight we found him, about 150 yards away, dead from a double-lung pass through. I was smitten with my new bow, but this was just beginning.

The next year we shot a 24" wide mule deer, a smallish 4 x 4 bull elk, and a few whitetail does. I still buy a pocketful of doe tags every year for two reasons. First, pan-fried alfalfa-fed whitetail doe backstraps are what I like to call "Montana lobster". Second, shooting does gives me live practice killing with my weapon, which I feel is absolutely priceless. My new Scorpion and I spent quite a bit of time thus practicing, and we were getting more and more comfortable with each other and becoming fast friends.

The epic bow season of 2007 was simply incredible. I started out with two beautiful archery killed caribou bulls in Quebec, and followed that with another heavy beamed 6-point bull elk on my very first morning out. A week later I shot an enormous 5x6 whitetail buck that grosses about 174 inches out of a rickety little ladder stand ratchet-strapped to a little juniper tree. In early October I killed my first ever archery antelope buck which measured a decent 14 inches. In addition I filled four whitetail doe tags that year and wrapped up the season with a javelina down in Arizona.

By now I was fully in love, and a true believer in this bow. Many hunting adventures now have variations on this basic story line. Animal arrives in range, I draw the Scorpion, anchor, settle the sight picture, pray condolences to the pre-dead target, release, hit, watch the animal run away mortally wounded, find it, tag it, and take it home. This is not to say that I have never missed with this bow. I have missed plenty of times and suffered many embarrassing failures, but over the years the miss percentage keeps going lower and the kill percentage higher and the trophies just keep piling up.

A couple of years later my grown boys were on their way out antelope hunting when the topic of my dear old bow came up. From what I heard, my oldest son Devin started trash-talking my bow, telling Jake and Brett that my bow is a "fossil" and that I should man up and get a proper bow, one that is super fast, quiet, and has no hand shock. Like his bow. As a career salesman I have fairly thick skin, and insults to my honor, intelligence, and heritage usually fall away like water off a duck's back. But trash my *bow?* My beloved *Scorpion?* Well, that hurts. I chalked it up to youthful ignorance in order to avoid bloodshed, and so I called Devin a few days later and coolly asked him how many big game animals his fancy-pants brand new bow had killed. His answer was two. My answer back was forty-nine. 49 to 2. That is a world class butt-whuppin' in any sport. Then I asked him how many Pope and Young quality animals his new bow had killed so far. Zero to nine for me. Boone and Crockett qualifiers? Not even close to my one. I then invited him to check E-bay for a PSE Scorpion if he wanted to hunt with real trophy getter. At first he laughed it off, but every time I get something I send the boys a picture message and a text that reads

"Fossil strikes again" or "What has your Fossil killed today?" I think he might be changing his mind.

But, Devin has a point in a way. By now my old Fossil friend was battered and battle scarred, and frankly looked more like a pawn shop bargain than the trustworthy slayer of all things cloven-hoofed. A few years ago I fell dragging out an antelope and broke the broadhead cover off the quiver. The archery shop in Butte had a top that fit but the camo pattern was different. I put the mis-matched top on anyway. Gives it character. I am on the fourth or fifth string, the second Ripcord rest, the third Black Gold sight, and she just keeps killing stuff for me. When Kim and I went to Africa in August of 2012, I never even considered a new bow. I was rewarded with seven species of African plains game, including a 56 inch Kudu and a dandy little Duiker that, egged on by my guide, I miraculously shot at 68 yards. When we got home I had another outstanding bowhunting year in Montana, including a 6x7 whitetail buck that grosses right at 160 and a 19" black bear. But I know it can't last forever.

The truth is I really don't know how it will end for the Scorpion Fossil. Maybe the next time I pull her back a limb will explode and that will be that. Maybe I will baby her along until we get 100 animals together and then I will retire her. Wouldn't that be something? One hundred big game animals with the same bow! I once considered getting my Scorpion bronzed in tribute, but I have decided against that. Instead I want her laid at my side in my pine box when I have finally tagged out and gone to the white light, just in case there is an archery season on the other side.

Then we can get to work on the second hundred.


*****


I peel the airline luggage tag off my bow case and flop it on the zebra rug in my office. Popping it open, I pile out some gear and the musty smelling hunting clothes. I unbuckle the straps and lift out my very trusty and very old PSE Scorpion, abused and battered but still perfectly functional. In fact, I had just flown home from a January bow hunt in Ohio where I killed a doe and a 149 inch 4X4 whitetail buck. Those two animals are numbers 100 and 101 that I have taken over the past twelve seasons with that PSE Scorpion.

Random memories come to me as I attach the quiver and replace the numbered arrows. The big bull elk in Utah that stomped in through the oak brush to 13 yards. The 15 inch antelope in Montana that I bow killed in frigid November, all decked out in hunter orange as rifle season was winding down. The perfect arrow through a tremendous 56” kudu bull at 35 yards in South Africa. The evening I filled all three of my whitetail doe tags out of the same stand. The big bison bull in Wyoming that fell to a single arrow. The second caribou bull in Quebec that ran off 50 yards and died while hundreds and hundreds more caribou clattered past me, including at least a dozen bulls bigger than the one I had just shot. The three grand Montana whitetail bucks on the wall that we call The First Presidency. The heavy horned red stag in the scrub of New Zealand that was so close I first heard the grass breaking as he chewed. And earlier this season a 335 inch bull elk in New Mexico and a scraggly bull moose in Idaho, and finally the magnificent buck in Ohio that I literally shot in the last 30 seconds of the last minute of the last day.

We often wonder what it would look like if it were somehow possible to resurrect those 101 animals and turn them loose in the 30 acre pasture behind the house. It would be quite a sight. You would see a pile of whitetails, including a Booner and another 5 Pope and Young quality bucks. There would be 11 branch antlered bull elk and a few cows, a bull moose, a big bison, a couple caribou bulls, 7 plains game species from South Africa, several pronghorn antelope, a bear, three different animals from New Zealand, a few medium mule deer bucks, and a javelina. You would also see a graying hunter carrying a beat up old bow.

Certainly my beloved PSE Scorpion has been in my hand for most of the best of my hunting life. But now it is enough. A dozen years and 101 animals. Five score and one. A bit of melancholy settles over me as I carefully retire my bow to the pelt rack in my office, step back, and give it a long, long salute…

The Scorpion came to me brand new in the spring of 2005 and, like the halo on an angel, a magical dose of good fortune glowed around that bow right out of the box. By the 2013 season I had killed 64 animals with the bow, and for the first time I seriously thought I could get 100 animals with my trusty PSE. Each season I would buy maximum doe tags and apply for bow hunts across the West, carefully noting each notched tag in my personal Big Game Hunting Log. I was lucky to draw tags and harvest trophies in Utah, Wyoming, New Mexico, and Idaho. My wife Kim and I took a gloriously successful trip to New Zealand in 2015 to help pad the books. Through all of this my old Scorpion was like an energizer bunny on PSE steroids, it just kept going and going, and I should mention that my Tru Ball release has also been with me all those years performing with remarkable toughness and consistency. So when the 2016 season started and I was at 94 animals, I secretly thought it would be a piece of cake to get it done this year as I had drawn a New Mexico elk tag and an Idaho moose tag to go with my usual pocket full of Montana permits.

Quite predictably, however, Montana's season ended I was stuck at 99 animals, but I had a savior. He is a wild-eyed bow hunting nut named Kevin Hilgenberg from Batavia, Ohio.

A few Septembers ago my son Devin was trolling through some archery posts on the internet and came upon one that read something like this: "We are two hardcore bowhunters from Ohio now in Philipsburg, Montana on our very first elk hunt. Been here three days and haven't seen an elk yet. The private land we had lined up is a bust so far. If anybody has any ideas please call." As Philipsburg is only 30 minutes away from our home town of Drummond, Devin called and set up a meeting at a restaurant with the two luckless hunters, presumably to get them to buy his lunch. On the way out the door I reminded him of the bodily harm he could look forward to if he sent them to any of our good spots.

By the end of the week, not only had they been to our good spots but Devin was going out with them and showing them how to hunt those spots. They got into elk, got a shot off, had some other close calls, and were generally hooked. Kevin is an orthopedic PA in Ohio and his friend Kyle is a former Army Ranger now doing detective work, and after I met them I was happy Devin was helping them out. They were getting up early and working their butts off, the type of guys that if we told them that eating raw hamburger for lunch would improve their chances of killing an elk, they would have gobbled up two helpings each. They went home from that trip bone tired but with that elk crazy look in their eyes and I knew they would be back.

Devin and Kevin have hunted together every year since and have become great friends. Kevin keeps tempting us with stories about the monster whitetail bucks he has back in Ohio and then he would email trail camera pictures of enormous bucks to back it up. When I found out that their archery season went clear into February, a ding went off in my head and I asked Kim for a plane ticket to Ohio for my Christmas present. I called Kevin and pretty much invited myself out to Ohio for a week in January. Kevin insisted that I stay at his house, eat dinner with his family, drive his pickup, use his trail cameras, and sit in his treestands. There was only one problem, but it was a major. The weather completely sucked. Before I got there the fields were frozen with a skiff of snow on the ground and deer movement had been great. Then it warmed up and rained and rained. By week's end there were little lakes of standing water in the fields and it felt like I was hunting in rice paddies. The wind was completely wrong for our preferred stand, so we resorted to plan B and then to plan C. I persisted despite the weather and finally killed a doe on day 6, and celebrated the long-awaited goal of 100 big game animals taken with my PSE Scorpion with a nice restaurant dinner.

The wind finally cooperated for the last day. We decided I should sit that evening where there had been two great bucks on camera recently, although almost exclusively at night. A super cool and super big drop-tine buck that we estimated to be in the mid-

150's and a wide 4 x 4 that Kevin nicknamed Texas. From the stand that evening the wind was better but the rain was still coming in spats. Four does fed by out of range and a spike buck came right under the tree. About 15 minutes before dark I saw the shadow of a deer flitting along the edge of the woods and join up with the does. It was the huge 4 x 4! And just like that he was gone. I sat quietly a long time and was literally reaching into my pocket to text Kevin the heartbreaking news about the fleeting glimpse of Texas when I heard some splashing out in the field. The four does were coming back. I grabbed my bow and finally, there was Texas, a hundred and fifty yards out in the field with a little 3 point. High, wide, handsome, and in no hurry whatsoever. He ambled into range just barely in time and we found him piled up at the edge of the field by flashlight a few hours later. He is 23 inches wide and tapes out right at 149 inches. A truly great buck, and big game animal 101 for my honored and trusty old PSE Scorpion. Five score and one, and the magical halo of good luck held out to the very end. But now the Scorpion is retired to the pelt rack. Like Devin had said a few years ago while trash talking the Scorpion, now it really was time to get a new bow, a super fast, super quiet, fancy pants bow.

I suppose this is where I should say that I did exhaustive research into the replacement for the old Scorpion, that I trolled the internet for information and specifications and reviews. I should say that I called all my hunting buddies and got their votes for this bow or that, that I put my mall shoes on and went shopping, test shooting every make and model, and that I spent hours making a list of pros and cons and things I liked and things I didn't. But that's not what happened. By a series of fortunate circumstances, I simply got another PSE.

There is something comforting about brand loyalty- I like the Toyota Tundra, 125 grain Muzzy broadheads, Diet Mountain Dew, and Victoria's Secret nighties. So, after reviewing the current offerings from PSE and getting some high level advice, I simply decided to stay in the PSE family and got a brand new PSE Evolve 35.

My friend Bill, who owns Big Sky Archery in Belgrade, Montana and who badgers me constantly about the glorious virtues of the newest bows, was standing next to me the first time I shot my new Evolve 35. I hooked up the release, drew the bow, anchored, and touched the trigger.

"Did it go off," I asked, holding out the follow through. I glanced down and the arrow was gone alright. Bill's face was split in a big grin.

Holy cow! Super smooth, lightning fast, whisper quiet, zero hand shock, with a great back wall. I shot it again and the second arrow was an inch from the first. Wow! This new bow ain't your Grandpa's old Scorpion that's for sure! And right then, for the first time since I retired my old bow to the pelt rack, I am really excited about going hunting with my PSE Evolve 35.

I still want my trusty Scorpion laid beside me in my casket, but now that I have the new Evolve 35 shooting darts, I'm quite relieved that I don't have to go to the white light and tag out to start on my next 100 big game animals. I don't have to die at all. I can get started opening day.

# STILLED AND QUIET

*"To every thing there is a season, and a time to every purpose under the heaven: A time to be born, and a time to die... A time to kill, and a time to heal" Ecclesiastes 3:1-3*

The snap of my bowstring startled the young bull elk. He crow-hopped sideways a step and whirled his head, his ears focused toward the cow and calf that were feeding out in the meadow, looking bewildered, alert and eyes scanning, as if waiting for some elk signal from the cow to bolt. Neither of us knew that my arrow, completely soaked in blood, was stuck into the frost-killed grass opposite the bull, having passed completely through him in the blink of an eye. I crouched frozen, or as frozen as possible, the surge of hunter's adrenaline from such a close and hopefully successful elk encounter giving my limbs a severe palsy.

Within a few minutes the cow and calf relaxed, went back to feeding, and edged out of sight on the walk. My bull eventually meandered behind a thicket of burgundy colored brush about 70 yards away and stopped. I glued my binoculars on the bull, and through the brushy haze I could only make out his head, neck, and smallish four-point antlers. For several minutes he simply stood, and occasionally I would see his horns swivel as he turned his head this way or that. All at once he bedded down, and for the first time I let myself relax. If I was patient and smart he would die right there. The shot looked to be fatal, a little high of perfect but still well within the chest cavity, and the fact that he was now bedded after a scant fifty yards confirmed my hope that this elk was soon going to be dead.

A fortunate opening in the trees allowed me to see the bull better after he bedded down. His rump was toward me, his front feet folded under at an angle to the left so that I could see the length of his body and one side of his face. I knew that inside the elk the tops of the lungs were turning a light pink, leaking blood internally into the ribcage, unable to re-oxygenate the blood, causing the heart to weaken. Had my broadhead hit him eight inches lower in the chest, this hemorrhage would have been swift and overpowering, and the bull would be dead already.

This elk wasn't dead yet, but he didn't seem to be in any pain either. His ears twitched and flopped absently, as if merely flicking flies away. His eye showed no alarm, no panic, no terror. In fact, this elk looked like he had just taken a double dose of allergy medicine and was getting really sleepy. Another twenty minutes or so and he seemed only sleepier, and I could see the tips of his antlers rocking gently sideways then upright then tipping again, his nose occasionally stretching out to the ground in front of him, his ears drooping. His would be a quiet, private death.

Without warning, the bull got to his feet. My blood went cold with what I can only say was fear, and I dropped my binoculars and quickly pulled another arrow off my quiver and nocked it. The elk stood wobbly, like a newborn horse, and for a moment I thought he might fall right back down. Somehow he got himself moving to my right. I guessed him to be 75 yards out when he came into an opening, a shot I would never take with a bow at an unwounded animal. I stood without caution to give me a better shooting lane, gapped my 40 yard pin over his back, and shot. Low. The bull stopped and stared right at me but even now, seeing me in plain view, showed no panic. No pain. No recognition. I nocked another arrow and gapped higher, this arrow hitting the elk a bit high and just behind the ribs. He never even flinched. He simply stood and stared, and just as I was about to shoot again, he turned his butt toward me and walked about ten yards to the edge of the trees and fell awkwardly, crashing sideways in a little knot of willows. Now all I could see of him was the crown of his head and his antlers. The antlers were still up, but it was plain to see he was losing strength. His head dipped up and down like a bobblehead doll, and then the antlers went sideways and were still. I suddenly noticed my arm shaking with fatigue, and realized that I had unconsciously been holding my bow out in front of me for the last many seconds. I was rattled and anxious, like a school boy being caught doing something wrong, afraid even now of his escape. I lowered my bow and raised the binoculars, breathing deep, calming down. When twenty minutes had passed since I had last seen the tips of his antlers move, I approached him.

He lay on his side, legs and neck outstretched, tongue out. Dead. Two blood stains on the golden hide over the ribcage marked the wounds, little pink bubbles frothing out the first. I knelt and twisted his antlers, the familiar smell of bull elk reconnecting a deep and mysterious circuit somewhere in my soul. I considered a moment the great mystery of the warmth ebbing from his body. Not only the warmth, but the entire organism, miraculously created and maintained and perpetuated by nothing more than the energy in plain old mountain grass. The meat and horns and hide and guts, all of it. Grass and water. But no amount of grass could help him now. His once shiny and knowing eyes were now dulled and empty. All his biological systems stilled and quiet.

*Well, buddy, you sure made it interesting.*

He had died well, if there is a way to judge such a thing, maybe better than I had killed. It was me, after all, the hunter, who had shown panic and fear on this morning. Maybe elk don't even have what we call panic and fear, or bewilderment or sleepiness or anything else. Maybe this bull showed no recognition of his dying because there was none. Maybe they simply live, filling the divinely appointed role of elk, consumed by the overwhelming instincts of the species to eat and rut and survive, perfectly incapable of existence in any other sphere.

I tugged the bull around and tucked in his tongue for some self-timer photos, and marveled as always at the exquisitely colored hide and antlers and hooves that are bundled up into the organism we call elk. It dawned on me that maybe I actually cheapen the miracle of this bull when I try to put human words into an elk's mouth and say with any certainty that he showed no fear or that he was bewildered or got sleepy, or that he died better than I killed. Maybe there is more meaning in measuring only myself and leaving it at that.

The September sun was overhead now, warming the air, and I broke a good sweat skinning and quartering the bull. An hour or so later the joy and thanksgiving of my bow-killed bull returned, the necessary tasks at hand having pushed out the troubling and the unanswerable.

*****

I peek up out of the clay creek wash, a dry prairie wind blowing hard into my face. At first I don't see any of the antelope, but then the back of a doe moves along the top of a sagebrush. Then another pokes out. They are much closer than I expected. I look down at John waiting in the bottom of the wash and grin. He inches up and props out his binoculars.

The antelope move along the sagebrush on the opposite rim of the wash, angling toward us. With great respect for the outrageous eyesight of these animals, I push my daypack in front of me in super slow motion and rest my rifle on it. In a few minutes the does are almost directly to my left across the wash, a small buck near the front. I wait for the bigger buck we'd seen earlier.

He appears out of a fold in the sage and trots to catch up, a few straggler does filtering in behind him. He is a decent trophy, maybe 14 inches, and I had already determined that I would take him if I got a chance. John had urged me to wait for one of the buster bucks we saw last year but this trip had come late in the season and I had some pressing issues at home. This buck would do fine.

We lay flat and undetected. I had a solid rest. The buck was well within a hundred yards. When he exposed the line behind his front shoulder, I centered the crosshairs and evenly pressured the trigger.

The whole herd of antelope sprinted away at the shot, a windy trail of dust chasing them in vain across the prairie. I quickly regained the buck in the scope, a circle of blood widening perfect behind his shoulder. He ran with the herd a few seconds, sprinting flat out, dodging and darting through the sagebrush, and then he piled up on his face in a cloud of dust, all four legs running in the air until he was still. The rest of the antelope kept going, roping out across the desert until they curled behind a bluff a mile away.

John looked over, grinned his approval, and we high-fived. After some pictures, we gutted the buck. The shot had been perfect, taking both lungs and the top of the heart. A good, clean kill.

Later, on the way home while John slept, I thought about the buck and how his legs kept running even after he was down. I wondered what it would be like to be an antelope and be shot through the heart and lungs. Eventually, it pleased me to think that the buck had simply heard a loud bang and then he ran and ran and ran right off the desert and ran for the bright white light and into the stars to the place where antelope run forever.

*****

I noticed that Dave had frost on his eyebrows when we topped the knob that would open the foothills into view. It was February and it was cold. An old-fashioned, Montana-style, butt-kicking cold. Being fairly new to Montana and elk hunting at the time, I had applied for and drawn this late season permit for an antlerless elk, assured that it was a great freezer-filling opportunity back in the spring when it was considerably warmer. I tested my own eyebrows. Flakes of ice showed in my glove.

The view through the bitter morning haze warmed us considerably. A couple miles off, long strings of elk meandered across the barren foothills leading to the mountains. The total number of elk had to be pushing at least five hundred and, of course, the closest elk to us were a group of big bulls, not legal to shoot but impressive nonetheless. We quickly formulated a stalk on the nearest herd of cows, marched across a flat and dropped into a little timbered draw, intending to circle out above the elk. We never got that far.

At the bottom of the draw, Dave froze. He looked just like a bird dog on point.

"I smell elk," he whispered.

In seconds, eight or ten smatterings of color crashed through the timber above us, angling down, and we heard them cross the bottom of the draw below us just out of sight. I looked at Dave wide-eyed.

"Run!" he barked.

I knew the country beyond was open and rolling, but I had to get out of the bottom of this draw to see it. I hustled up the hill, pushing myself well beyond my aerobic capacity, and crested the ridge. I was expecting to see the elk as little golden dots moving on the horizon. Even I knew enough about elk hunting to know that when it turns into a foot race, you lose. This time, however, the elk were single-filing up toward a little ridge a couple hundred yards away. The lead cow had just disappeared out of sight when I shot at the last cow in line, the report of the gun tinny and hollow in the arctic air.

I was breathing hard and in a hurry and took the shot offhand even though I knew better and hit her just above the knee joints in the hind legs. The next shot, also taken standing up, missed entirely. The cow kept laboring up the hill, despite two broken hind legs, and I could feel myself winding up in a big knot of panic.

*Get a grip on yourself and get this elk!*

I sat deliberately in the snow, resting my elbows on my knees, and the elk's chest quit wobbling so bad in the scope. At the next shot, I heard the *thwok* of a solid hit. The next shot felt good too, but I didn't know for sure. I scrambled for more bullets and reloaded my rifle, trying way too hard to do it fast, and finally fumbled the fourth cartridge into the magazine and slammed the bolt.

When I got the cow back in the scope she was still up, splay-legged, and seemed to be working hard not to go down. I shot.

"Nice one. Hit her again!"

Dave's voice from below startled me, but I focused and shot again. And once more. Somehow the old cow stayed up, soaking up the lead, and then she finally folded her front legs under her and plopped down in the snow.

In the scope, I saw her swing her head down and thought she was done, but then she stretched her nose straight into the sky and her head fell backwards over her front shoulders and she bellowed out a guttural, grunting cry. In that very instant, her whole frame sagged and her legs stiffened and she slid a ways down the hill. It was a haunting finale, and I knew I had witnessed the exact moment when the life or spirit or ghost or whatever you want to call it had departed that elk. She had not gone gently.

"Oh yeah, you got her. Nice shooting. Tough old buggers aren't they?"

Dave was by my side, jabbering, and I was genuinely relieved it was over. It was too cold to sit around and theorize much, so we got to work on gutting and quartering her. Dave reached over and pulled on a hind leg, noticed it was broken above the joint and looked at me, frowning. He obviously hadn't cleared the draw in time to see all of it.

"First shot," I said simply.

"Well, luckily it didn't waste much meat."

We opened her up and gutted her. Bullet holes riddled the inside the ribcage, and one of the shots had hit high in the neck. We finished quartering her, and put the pieces meat-side down and covered the hide with snow to keep the birds off, tying some surveyors tape onto a nearby tree to help locate the spot when we came back with the horses. We packed a few handfuls of the sugary snow and rubbed them over our hands and wrists, bloody droplets pocking the snow at our feet.

"Kind of freaky how she groaned like that," I said, pulling my gloves back on.

"Never heard one do that before," Dave said. "She wouldn't let go, that's for sure."

The next afternoon when we checked out at the Fish and Game trailer, the biologist estimated her age at 10 years old, mentioning that she was an old, dry cow and that from the wear on her teeth she probably would have starved to death and not made it through the winter anyway, and that at the very least I had saved her from that. I pictured her nose again in the air, outstretched, her head dropping over her shoulders, that piercing groan delivering her to the unseen and I truly hoped I had done her well.

*****

It's Christmas vacation 1984, and I am in California to meet the people who will become my in-laws and my by-marriage relatives. One of Kim's sisters-in-law, Lisa, a lukewarm animal lover, starts in on me about hunting and, being outnumbered, I try to pass it off with a little humor.

"How can you shoot those poor, defenseless deer? What have they ever done to you?" she asks.

"Well, you have to hold the rifle real steady and gently squeeze the trigger. Squeeze the trigger, don't jerk it mind you, and..."

"That's not what I mean," she interrupts. "What I mean is, what do you think all those deer are going to say to you when you get to heaven?"

"Well, I hope they say, 'Nice shot'!"

My future father-in-law Grandpa Dean grins slightly, and Kim gives me the look that means that it might be a good idea to change the subject.

2

Twenty years and around eighty big game kills later and I have quit thinking the whole heaven scenario to be so far fetched, and my hope has truly and sincerely grown that if they can, those animals will say to me exactly that.


*****


A greenish "V" expands out and down my lane in the freeway, followed by the crumpled remains of a deer rolled out to the guardrail. Dead-centered by an eighteen wheeler by the looks of it. I see this scene and others like it dozens of times a year on the highways here in Montana, the carcasses of the road killed deer in various stages of mangle and bloat, most of them victims of the proverbial deer-in-the-headlights. Once in a while I wonder why an animal whose instincts make it so elusive, so incredibly sensitive to scent and movement and disturbance, why an animal with all those defenses and instincts, so difficult to stalk up on in the woods, why a deer like that would just run out on the pavement and let a truck run it over.


*****

We left the kids in the International Scout with instructions to honk the horn if they got scared or needed anything. Kim had drawn an antlerless mule deer tag and we had spotted a lone doe feeding on the hillside a short distance above the Forest Service road. A couple of minutes later I watched through the binoculars as Kim shot across the canyon. It looked perfect, and the deer bolted downhill dragging its front shoulder in the death run and disappeared into the timber. Seconds after the shot the horn honked. Kim gave me the concerned mommy look.

"Go ahead," I said. "I'll go gut the deer and pull it to the road. Drive down a ways and I'll whistle and you can come and find me. Bring the kids."

I dropped off the hill and hiked up the other side to where the doe stood. There was good blood and a fluff of hair where the wandering line of tracks abruptly bounded downhill. I tracked confidently into the timber, looking ahead for the skid mark in the snow where the doe would have piled up. Instead, I saw the flit of a live deer disappear uphill through the trees.

*Must be a different deer.*

But the blood tracked right to the place where I saw the deer bolt, and now she was going uphill. Bad news, but there was still good blood and good snow. It wouldn't take long.

The horn honked from below and I knew the kids would be anxious to get in on our deer hunt. The tracks continued uphill, then across a little draw, then uphill again. Distantly the horn honked again. The blood on the track started to peter out, and I began to wonder if my eyes had betrayed me. I replayed my view of the shot in my mind, the doe standing still, slightly quartering towards us, ears wide, studying us across the hill, a dust of hair as the bullet strikes low at the bend of the shoulder and caves it, the deer kicking out with both hind legs and running straight downhill with its tail tucked.

I thought about the bullet striking the deer, like one of those frame-by-frame movies of a bullet going through an apple. I knew that the bullet left the gun at a hair over 3000 feet per second, spiraling like a football from the rifling inside the barrel. I estimated the yardage at somewhere around 150 yards, 450 feet, the bullet crossing that space in just over a tenth of a second. Upon impact, the soft lead center of the bullet would expand, mushrooming to approximately twice its original diameter, held together by the outer copper jacketing. As the bullet pierced the hair and hide and entered the shoulder tissue, the energy from the velocity and the mass of the bullet would begin to transfer into the deer. The bullet would blast through the shoulder bone, perhaps fragmenting slightly, and continue tunneling a channel through the lungs and other internal tissues. Immediately, a dramatic hemorrhage would begin inside the ribcage, which would become the ultimate cause of biological death. The bullet would be slowing by now, the energy transfer nearly complete, and if the bullet's performance were perfect it would break a rib on the way out and come to rest mashed against the inside of the hide on the far side of the deer in a little blood-shot bruise. All of this happening so fast that it is unusual to even see it as a puff of hair on the shoulder and is over long before the sound of the blast fades.

I jumped the deer once more in the timber, but got no shot, the doe still dragging her useless front shoulder. I was tiring myself, and as I wiped the sweat off from under my hat I realized that I'd been steady on the track well over an hour by now. Probably a solid mile anyway. The deer had circled me uphill and across the face of some timber and was now back on the ridge we had originally shot from. I knew Kim would be sick with worry, but I had no choice but to try and finish this here and now.

A few minutes later, and with no warning, the doe jumped up in front of me and my rifle came to arms and I found the base of her neck in the scope just as she disappeared over the curve of the hill. The shot echoed. The smell of burnt gunpowder and snow hung heavy. I found her piled up dead, eyes bugged out weirdly from the cranial shock of my gunshot hitting her at the base of the skull. Right off I noticed how small she was. Actually, a he, the antlerless deer being a three-quarters grown buck fawn. I bent down and brushed off the chunks of blood ice on the front shoulder and pulled the broken leg back. I blew through my teeth in amazement and awe. Kim's bullet had totally destroyed the lower front shoulder and had opened up a nasty gash in the brisket, but had missed the heart by a mere inch or two. I absolutely could not believe this little deer had pushed so far and so valiantly with such a devastating wound.

I patted the tiny buck, a profound respect surging in me for such a big will to live inside such a small deer. I stood on the ridge and whistled for the kids, taking a moment to re-trace our tracks through the mountains, shaking my head, an odd feeling welling in me that I had witnessed something extraordinary. Actually, that I had participated in something extraordinary. I puzzled at myself for giving this little deer valiance and will, normally refusing to allow myself to wax anthropomorphic, but I truly felt a heightened energy from the chase and kill and discovery of this deer. Although too little to even have horns, this deer seemed to be a trophy in a more pragmatic way. Pragmatic but undefinable, and all I could do was hope the eating of him might strengthen my own heart and give courage to my own will to live.

*****

Big, downy snowflakes parachuted softly through the trees, darkening the gathering darkness, gloomy and magnificent all at the same time. This year's buck lay gutted and tagged, the snow gathering on his hide and on my daypack. Of course the deer had run straight downhill at the shot and died in a pick-up-sticks pile of blown down lodgepole. Of course I'd have to drag him back up and over the ridge to get him out. Nevertheless I was pleased. There had been a good measure of hunt in this hunt, and the shot had been perfect. Both lungs, low and lethal. A "nice shot" type of shot.

I brushed the snow out in a wide circle around my daypack, looking for my knife sheath or saw case or any other stray gear. The gut pile remained dark against the white forest floor, the last of the deer's body heat refusing for the moment to succumb to the snow.

For whatever mysteries remain, I am confident of this - that the killing of a deer is more than simply the ceasing of its biological functions. More than simply shutting off the furnace. More than dust to dust. There is too much mystery, too much spirit, too much that beckons and pulls in the final seconds when a deer becomes venison for it to be otherwise. The fact that the snowless gut pile on the forest floor would be eerily similar to my own seems to me a clue, but hazy and incomplete like most of the other clues.

Darkness hadn't quite gathered completely, and the new snow gave the forest floor contrast. I'll probably make it out before pitch black, but I dug the flashlight out of my daypack and dropped it in the cargo pocket of my pants anyway. Looking straight up into the charcoal gray sky, the snowflakes seemed to appear out of the dark just above the pine boughs, flutter into view for a moment, and then drift onto the forest floor. So much like us. From out of an indefinable black void stream infinite numbers of slightly individual snowflakes, each fluttering in a slightly individual journey, each unavoidably destined for oblivion on the forest floor. I squinted my eyes into the flakes for a few minutes, catching some on my tongue like a school boy.

The edges of the gut pile were beginning to take snow when I looped my drag strap over the deer's neck and halter hitched his nose. I faced the buck, dug in my heels, and pulled. Stepped back, dug in my heels, and pulled again. The buck would be heavy going uphill and darkness had nearly swallowed up the snowy forest night, gloomy and magnificent all at the same time.

# GONE WHERE?

*"Blessed are they that mourn: for they shall be comforted"*
*Matthew 5:4*

I glance at the clock and grimace. Almost three in the afternoon and only half of the day's work list is checked off in my day planner. I pile the papers on my desk and ditch out of the office anyway, gas up, and drive up the canyon and out of cell range. The early September afternoon is border-line hot, and I reach down and punch the air conditioning on. Archery season is barely a week old and it's been less than a month since my mother's sudden and unexpected death. The weeks in between have been almost impossibly hectic and, as I face my palms to the air cooling out of the dashboard vents, I reach over and shut off the babbling radio. A few minutes later I turn the air conditioning off and roll all the windows down, the Montana afternoon blowing through the cab and tousling my hair. Much better. The pavement changes into gravel with a bump, a tunnel of dust trailing my truck. With finally a minute to itself, my mind wanders absently in circles of work to be done and memories of Mom and, almost by accident, to shooting a deer with my bow this evening. But there is no surge, no anticipation. Right now I need something more than a deer, but I'm not sure exactly what. Maybe some clean Montana air and some quiet. Maybe just the quiet.

Kim and I were in Missoula on a Saturday morning returning a rented fence post-pounder when we got the news. Mom had come home from the hospital after what was supposed to be routine shoulder surgery, but she had suffered a rough night when the nerve block wore off about midnight. After a little breakfast she finally got to sleep and just never woke up. A little after 9:00, Dad noticed that she wasn't breathing and tried to get her to come around but she wouldn't wake up and then he called my brother who lives down the road in a panic. When my brother got there he took one look and he knew. The emergency people came too, but she was gone. And that's the first thing my brother told me on the cell phone. That Mom was gone.

I said, "Gone where?"

I park at the corner of the fence and change into my hunting clothes behind the open passenger door of the pickup. I shoulder my daypack and grab my bow, straddle over the barbed wire fence and am about a hundred yards down the ditchbank before I realize I left my binoculars on the dashboard. I set my bow down in the tall grass and trot back to get them, cursing my absent-minded self. The afternoon is brilliant and sky-blue, the surrounding mountains all fancied up in their autumn splendor. I gather my bow and walk along an edge of tall grass to my treestand and jump a whitetail doe and fawn out of the ditch bank. The fawn is barely out of its spots and both deer leapfrog away, sleek and graceful. They stop and pause for a second look and high-step away, their white tails flagging back and forth. When I get to the aspen tree, I climb out of my daypack and up the treestand. I adjust the seat a bit before pulling my bow up. The golden yellow leaves on the tree bustle and wobble in the breeze and it smells like aspen bark and fall. I draw in several full breaths of air and shut my eyes and tilt my face to the sun for a minute or two, settling in. A couple of well used deer trails cross in front of me well within bow range at the edge of the hayfield. I choose an arrow with a brand new broadhead and nock it, and hang the bow from a lopped off aspen limb.

On the second pass across the hay field with my binoculars, I notice a dark bump in a clump of tall grass out near the wheel line. I focus on it for a minute or two and when it moves again I can see it is a coyote waking up from his afternoon nap. He sits up on his haunches, focused on something in the grass in front of him, and after a few minutes he stands up, stretches, and trots off in zig-zags.

He is maybe a couple of hundred yards off, but coming closer at an angle that might put him right under my stand. Even I am surprised that I couldn't care less.

Kim and I hurried home from Missoula to gather up, but we had to wait for our two daughters Holly and Jessi, who were actually on their way home from Rigby, having spent the past three days helping put the roof on Mom and Dad's new house. When Holly had stopped by earlier that morning to say goodbye, Grandma was up having a little breakfast and nobody could have ever imagined that their short conversation and hug out the door would be Mom's last. By late afternoon, we had made the four hour drive to Idaho. All the rest of the family was already there too, everybody dropping everything to be there and do what they could. A tangible sadness permeated the house, and my Dad was so broken up that I truly worried that he might not make it through the night himself. The next day, I sat at the computer and compressed all the suggestions into an obituary for the newspaper. We gathered at the table to plan the funeral and Dad would sit in for a minute or two, then he would leave and then he would return, dabbing at his forehead with a damp cloth, then he would leave again.

That evening, all the adults except Dad went to the mortuary to order the programs and buy a casket. A reverent quiet filled the reception area of the funeral home but it felt tragic and dull, the walls of the place lingering with grief. I thought it odd when I noticed that there were a couple of vacation travel magazines displayed on the coffee table. The funeral home director, Brother Eckersell, a man who goes to the same church we grew up in and who our family has known for a long time, guided us past a hallway office of computers and file cabinets and pictures of kids thumbtacked to the cubicles. He showed us into the casket display room and patiently showed us the different models and prices and colors and that was when my sister Amy's emotions ran her over. At first we settled on a less expensive bronze-colored casket, but then had second thoughts and got a pure white one with metallic roses on the corners. None of it seemed real anyway.

Somewhere along the way, Dad told us how Mom came out of her surgery. The nurse came out and found Dad in the waiting area and said the surgery had gone well but that Mom had asked for him. Still in and out of it, her eyes fluttering open and shut, she asked Dad when the people were going to quit singing. Dad assured her that nobody was singing. Yes, she said, people were singing and had been for a while and not only that but Gramps was there and some other people too and they told her it was time to come with them but she wouldn't. At the time, he chalked it up to the anesthesia. She never mentioned it again, but throughout the day she was unusually adamant about going home right away. By afternoon she seemed to be doing remarkably well, and when Kim talked to her on the phone Friday afternoon she mentioned to me that my Mom hadn't seemed that chipper for a long time. The doctor released her and Dad brought her home Friday night. I couldn't help but wonder if the people were singing again when Gramps came back.

Gramps is my mother's grandfather who had died back in the early 1970's. About all I can remember of him as a boy was that his favorite horse was a jet black stallion named King and that all the grandkids and great grandkids sang "Abide With Me 'Tis Eventide" at his funeral. In the spring of 1987, my maternal Grandmother was in a hospital and we were taking turns sitting with her and monitoring the blood oxygen machine. During one of my brother's shifts the number fell dramatically and he rang the bell for the nurse. Then the number on the monitor rose for a moment and Grandma opened her eyes at the ceiling and said, "Louise! Gramps!" Then she died, just like that. Louise being Grandma's half sister that had passed away a few years before, and Gramps is evidently the President of our family's Grim Reaper Committee, and I am somewhat perplexed by the powerful yearning inside that pulls me to simply believe all of it.

Mom had made it known previously that she wanted a closed casket funeral and no family viewing after her passing, preferring for us to remember her in life and not in death. Nevertheless, it ate away at Dad until he finally admitted that he wanted to go in to the mortuary and see her before the funeral. Jason and I volunteered to go in with him but he said he wanted to go by himself and disappeared into the garage. Twenty seconds later he came back, and without a word the three of us piled into the car. When we opened the door into the funeral home I noticed that the travel magazines were in exactly the same place on the coffee table. Dad went into the viewing room alone and came out a scant few moments later, all teary-eyed and sniffling. Then Jason and I went in. The room was softly lit and shadowy, the casket with the roses situated against the far wall with the lid open. Kim and my sister-in-law Jolyn had come in the day before and done Mom's hair and makeup and she looked nice. Peaceful and still. I brushed her hand with mine, the exact same hand which had through the years wiped the tears off my cheeks and paddled my bottom and wrote me letters and waved goodbye and hugged my children. It was cold and solid. She was dead. Go ahead and put that cold old clay in the ground because my Mom wasn't in there. She wasn't anywhere. Like my brother had said, Mom's gone.

I was asked to speak at the funeral and that's when I lost it, a knot tying up my throat barely into the first paragraph. I sobbed out the rest of my remarks and after that the rest of the funeral kind of blurred. While the white casket was being carried by the grandsons from the church to the hearse, my eleven year old daughter Jessi timidly asked if Grandma was really in there. The question caught me off guard, and I glanced up at Kim, tears brimming in her eyes. How the hell do you answer a question like that? We eventually said yes, that Grandma was in there. What was left of her anyway.

I lean into the aspen, keeping an eye on the coyote. He's closer now, maybe a hundred yards. He eases to a stop, gathers himself, and springs about three feet in the air. Probably at a mouse, but he must have missed. Unfazed, he keeps prowling back and forth, coming my way until the breeze changes directions and touches the back of my neck. The coyote slams to attention, nose in the air, and it turns and runs full speed clear out of sight.

An hour later, I catch the movement of a doe hopping a fence a quarter mile away, back toward my pickup. She stands like a statue for several minutes and then, with a flick of her tail, she relaxes and feeds into the alfalfa. Within thirty minutes there are seven or eight more deer in the field, including a couple small bucks. I glass beyond the deer to the spectacular Montana mountains, burgundy and canary and green, and know without seeing that in those mountains the bull elk are starting to bugle and the mule deer bucks are stripping the velvet off their antlers. A little finch flits over my head and disappears into a knothole, hops out, jumps to a different limb, and flies off. A few minutes later from somewhere behind me a line of geese honk their way down the river.

*Gone where?*

Night inches its way in, and the evening painting is spectacular. Pastel purples and pinks trailing the sun to the west. Speckles of stars in the east. A cooling thermal rattles the golden aspen leaves around my treestand and rustles the grass on the ditchbank. I catch myself breathing evenly in and out, listening. Waiting. Asking.

*In the pastels of the sunset? Into the stars? In the breeze that wobbles the leaves? In the air I'm breathing? Where are you?*

Without ever checking my watch, I sit still in the stand until way past shooting light. Not one deer came closer than those in the alfalfa field. No deer, and despite the quiet and my earnest searchings there would be no answer either, except for maybe the thought that sooner or later Gramps will come for me and I'll get to find out for myself. But there were no revelations. No quiet whispers. No spiritual wave of comfort or peace. Nothing supernatural, except for the natural setting of a bluebird September afternoon. Nothing extraordinary, other than the ordinary comings and goings of splendid Montana autumn.

I sit unmoving in my stand until it is almost completely dark. I stand up for a few minutes on the platform of my stand, still listening and waiting, not wanting to go but not wanting to stay either. Finally, I lower my bow to the ground, climb out of the tree and stretch. I decide that I am feeling a little better anyway. Maybe a little bit healed. Walking back to the truck, the night is nearly dark and I have to watch my steps and walk real slow along the ditchbank. Closer to the truck, I can barely make out the wagging white tails of the deer bounding out of the field ahead of me. I make a mental note of the fact that the deer hopped out of the field at the same spot in the fence they came in from, and I am pretty sure I could get one if I set up right there when I come back in a day or two.

# GIVE AND TAKE

*"In the morning sow thy seed, and in the evening withhold not thine hand: for thou knowest not whether shall prosper, either this or that, or whether they both shall be alike good."*
*Ecclesiastes 11:6*

L ittle Jacob was the first to say it.

"So, Dad, what happens if the world record buck comes out and Devin has the gun?"

"Well," I shrugged, adjusting the rifle slung across my shoulder. "I'll grab it from him, kill that world record buck, and hurry and give it back just in case a little buck comes out later."

Devin shot me a frowning glance, eyebrows furrowed.

I had wrapped up my work day a couple hours early and darted out to get Devin and Jacob from an after-school Boy Scout activity, although there wasn't time to get all the way home first to gear up. We would have to make do with my gun. No big deal. Even though I had my tags in my daypack, the main reason for this hunt was to get Devin a chance at a nice whitetail buck. He was 13, and in his second year of hunting. Jacob was too young to hunt, but too wild-eyed to stay home. So it ended up that the three of us were ambling up an old farm road along the edge of an alfalfa field, about to set up in an irrigation ditch by a corner of the river bottom for the evening deer hunt. Three people, two hunters, and one gun.

Montana's rifle season was in its third day, and the late October afternoon had bloomed golden and warm. We found that the ditch still had a little standing water in it, but we eventually found a reasonably dry spot and broke the grass down on the ditchbank for a better view. I was situating everything when Devin timidly asked for the gun, just to make sure he could see into the field through the scope. I smiled and carefully handed him the gun. He pointed the gun out to the field, leaned into the ditch bank, and squinted into the scope, adjusting his rear end a time or two. He looked up and nodded, but made no motion to give the gun back.

Jacob kept pestering Devin about whether or not he was going to hold out for a forked-horn this year. The year before, Devin's first year, the three of us were waiting at the edge of a different field for Devin's very first buck. Just before dark a whitetail deer came into the field and nibbled its way toward us until it was no more than 40 yards away. A spike buck, but it was a tiny little thing and had one of it's horns broken off. A one-horned spike. Devin looked at me and whispered, "What do you think?"

"It's legal and it's your tag. Your call," I shrugged.

"C'mon Devin shoot it!" Jake begged in a whisper. "Look how close it is. Not even you could miss it! Shoot!"

Devin gritted his teeth and looked at the buck in the scope. Then he put the gun down, then up again.

He looked over at me and whispered again, "Do you think we can find a bigger one later?"

His eyes were begging me to say no.

"Actually, it would be nearly impossible not to find a bigger one."

"Shoot him. Shoot!" Jake whispered in a frenzy.

Finally the deer ran off, and Devin ended up shooting a two-horned spike later in the season for his first buck. We often tease Devin that he is quite the trophy hunter since he held out for a two-horned spike for his first buck.

"So what do you think," Jake pestered. "You gonna shoot a forked horn?"

"Shut up," Devin said.

"All right, that's enough. You guys chill out and be quiet."

The easy breeze went cooler as the sun set, and a few little groups of ducks winged along the river, their wings whistling in the air above us. Even the boys impatiently quieted down some. The hunting half hour was upon us.

Since Devin still had the gun propped out in front of him, I kept busy glassing the brush lines for deer movement. I had just swung my field of view to the far end of the field and was starting back when I saw an elk as big as day in the binoculars.

"Elk!" I hissed.

The boys stiffened and craned their necks toward the field, eyes bugging out of their heads.

*Elk! Holy Smokes!*

While I knew that elk hit this area once in a while, I had not expected to see them here today. Usually they are in the area during early archery season, drawn to the green feed, but once rifle season hits they get pushed into more remote areas. I took quick mental stock of the situation. I had a tag for a brow-tined bull. Devin had a cow permit.

"Get ready," I whispered.

A few seconds later about 30 elk started spilling out of the brush and grazing on the alfalfa. The very first elk to show itself was a bigger than average five-point bull. He jumped into the field, his cream and chocolate hide glowing in the last light of evening, and he plodded right at us until he was only about 60 yards away. He stopped and turned broadside, the tips of his antlers bobbing as he grazed, and I could actually hear the grass stems break as he chewed them off. All the other elk were cows and calves and spikes, but they hung back against the edge of the field 200 yards away. I swung the binoculars back to the bull, his magnified image absurdly large, and watched him munch away with my very own disbelieving eyes.

Keep in mind that over the years I have suffered all manner of hunger, thirst, and fatigue in the mostly fruitless search for bull elk. I had forfeited wages from missed work, gone into debt for vehicles I didn't otherwise need, and neglected countless responsibilities and commitments in the quest for antlered elk. Much of our scant discretionary income went for things like bullets and camo pants and tire chains. I paid in other ways too. Once I came home from an elk hunt and noticed that we had new furniture, Kim grinning and shrugging her shoulders when I noticed. Many pairs of boots have been dumpstered after untold miles of tortuous scrabbling in the hard country looking for an elk exactly like the one that now stood so close I could hear it chew. A five-point bull elk, broadside, grazing on alfalfa 60 yards away! A whole freezer full of elk steaks and elk burger and elk roasts, standing there like a big old five-point Christmas present! I peeked down the ditch at the gun barrel pointed into the field.

"Devin," I said out the corner of my mouth, barely audible. "Hand me the gun so I can shoot this bull, and then I'll get it right back to you."

"I'm already lined out on a cow," he said staring into the rifle scope, his voice shivering with excitement. I hesitated a second, knowing full well the consequence of my next sentence.

"OK, shoot the cow," I said, moving the binoculars to the string of cows. "Which one?"

He shot without answering, and I heard the *thwop* of a hit. The bull bolted and the other elk started milling around and running, and then I saw a cow standing splay-legged, head drooping, looking gut shot.

"Shoot her again," I said out loud.

Boom!

"Again!"

Boom! Boom!

Seven shots in all until the old cow's legs buckled and she hit the ground on her

side. I stood up and bellered out a big victory whoop and jumped up to give Devin a high five. He looked up from the gun, his eyes the size of silver dollars, his face all contorted in a wide smile that showed adrenaline and excitement and pure relief all at the same time. He and Jake were jabbering nonstop as we made our way out to the dead elk. We gutted her out in the fading light, and Ron, the landowner, even drove out to help us load her into the pickup.

Later that evening, when things had quieted down some, Devin showed up at my side.

"Hey Dad," he said, digging his toe into the carpet. "I was thinking that maybe I should have given you the gun to shoot that bull since a bull is way harder to find than a cow."

"No, you did the right thing. I told you to shoot and you shot. We got an elk out of the deal and besides, now you are done hunting elk for the year but I still have my tag. You did great. I'll just have to make sure to bring two guns next time."

This seemed to please him some, and he disappeared into his room. Later, as I lay in bed, the view of that five-point bull standing broadside at 60 yards replayed itself in my mind over and over, and I had to force myself to wish away the regrets of that lost opportunity with the picture of Devin's face when the old cow finally dropped.

*But still, 60 yards broadside!*

I finally talked myself into just being happy for Devin, pulled the covers up, and went to sleep.

And, wouldn't you know it, the very next afternoon I went down to the same place and right before dark I shot my very first six-point bull.

*****

I untied my soggy wading boots and tipped them upside down on the parking lot, a small puddle of water edging across the pavement as they drained. I hung my waders from the rear view mirror of the rented Ford Explorer and sprawled across the passenger seat with the door open, trying to air out some and rest my eyes. I was at the Pink Salmon parking lot on the Russian River in Alaska, enjoying some sockeye salmon fishing with Devin and his friend Jordan. They had graduated from high school the previous May, and this trip was their long-anticipated graduation present. Jordan's dad Tom had also planned to come but some persistent knee troubles caused him to back out at the last minute, and so just the three of us made the trip to Anchorage. On the calendar was some sockeye fishing on the Russian, a day on the ocean for halibut, and a week long float through the wilds of Alaska for King Salmon.

We stopped at a sporting goods store in Anchorage to get our fishing licenses and propane bottles and Devin showed up in the checkout line with a little tiny $7.99 kids Snoopy pole, announcing that he was not only going to catch a King Salmon on that pole but record the whole event on video. I had personally seen the mighty King Salmon ruin plenty of high-dollar equipment, let alone a Snoopy pole. I smiled as I thought of watching Devin yanking back with that little pole, setting the hook on a King. There would be a momentary pause and then the line would scream out of the drag for a couple seconds and then there would be an explosion of gears inside that little reel that would sound like marbles in a food blender. Driving to the Russian River, Jordan and Devin decided to take the Snoopy pole on a trial run with the sockeyes, just to kind of get the feel of it. I smiled again and wagged my head. This was going to be quite the trip.

When we got to the Russian we found out that we had missed the early surge of migrating fish, and that first afternoon there were only a few stragglers here and there. We still caught several, but Jordan and Devin stuck with their regular rods. Late the next morning, however, strings of hundreds of sockeyes kept finning past us and the fishing was terrific. Pretty soon I saw Devin appear down the bank, working the Snoopy pole and Jordan wading along behind, working the video camera. Once I saw the rod bend level and then the tip whipsaw back as the line broke. Devin turned around with a big grin on his face and mouthed something into the camera. I knew that they wouldn't quit until they caught one. I already had my limit and was worn out besides, so I plodded past the other fishermen on the river and up the trail to the Explorer to take a little rest.

I nodded off for a while and woke up when Jordan started rummaging around the coolers for some food. Devin came up minutes later, yakking and laughing, and the two of them started to rewind the video to show me the footage of the sockeye salmon he had landed with the Snoopy pole. Years of losing various outdoor gear and tools and such has taught me to take a quick inventory when the boys show up. They had the video camera, their fly rods, the spinning rod, their fish, their waders and their tackle boxes.

"Hey, Devin, where's your Snoopy pole?" I asked, expecting to hear the tale of its spectacular demise.

"I gave it to that little girl down by the river."

"You did what?"

"Yeah, you know, that family down by that little pool just below the stairs. I saw that little girl and her brother playing by the edge of the river with some stick poles so I said, 'Do you want a real fishing pole' and she said 'yes' so I gave it to her. I even left the fly on it."

"Just like that?" I asked.

"Yeah, just like that."

I made the off-handed comment that this was bound to please the fishing gods and bring him good luck and sure enough, the very next day out on the ocean, Devin landed a 176 pound halibut.

*****

My son Jacob and I were driving up a gravel road in my pickup, windows down, music up, leaving a tunnel of dust behind us in the warm September afternoon on our way to an evening of bow hunting. Rounding a corner, a minivan came into view ahead of us, stopped off to the side of the road. A couple of older ladies were out on the road gawking at the back of the vehicle. I eased off the gas and noticed as we coasted by that the van had Missoula license plates on it and a completely flat rear tire. One of the ladies kept punching numbers into a cell phone. I pulled off the road behind their van and started the flashers.

"May we be of assistance to you fine young ladies?" I asked dramatically.

"Well, I need to call my husband because we have a flat tire," one of the ladies said somewhat flatly, no doubt concerned about our appearance due to our hunting clothes.

"Ma'am, there is no cell service in this area and even if there was, calling your husband is a bad idea as me and my son Jake here are in a much better position to change this tire, assuming you have a spare. It would be our privilege to help you as we are on our way to go bowhunting and this will surely bring us good luck."

"I'm pretty sure there is a spare," she said, warming slightly.

"Then we will do our best."

We dug the spare out and got to work and we even got them to smile a time or two as we talked back and forth while the tire was changed.

"What can we pay you," one of the ladies asked quite sincerely when we were finished.

"Ma'am," I replied again with high drama. "Your money is no good to us and we are offended at your offer. Well, at least I am. It has simply been our pleasure to have been in your company for these few moments." Then I winked at her.

The lady smiled a half-smile, not sure if she had run into Sheriff Andy Griffith or Jeffrey Dahmer.

In another minute they drove away, leaving their own tunnel of dust back toward Missoula. Jake and I high-fived and grinned at each other like a pair of wolves who had just found a freshly shorn three-legged sheep. We piled into the truck and sped off toward our hunting area, so sure that this would bring us good luck that we even toyed with the idea of pre-notching our deer tags for that very day.

We parked the truck, hiked to our treestands, and waited until the sun went down and neither of us had a deer come close.

*****

Hoping to finish in time to squeeze in an evening hunt, I spent the lunch hour shuffling the pile of neglected paperwork on my desk. I had outwardly blamed my procrastination on being busy chasing the kids' ball games and such, but the real reason the reports were not done was that my un-notched elk tag was still in my daypack instead of hanging on the horns of a nice bull. The meat supply in the freezer was dwindling rapidly and the pressure was mounting. The calendar showed me that we were well into the third week of Montana's rifle season, week three out of five, and it had been one of those frustrating years when I would drag myself back to the truck after another exhausting hunt and I would look at the scope on the top of my rifle and I would wonder if I was ever going to see elk hair through those lenses again.

Toward the bottom of the pile of papers was a quarterly tax document, and I had highlighted a number on that paper to remind me to record a dividend we had taken in connection with the tax payment. While I was recording the dividend in the checkbook, I abruptly wondered if I had made the appropriate tithing donation at church on that income. A quick glance into my records showed that I had not, but since the amount of money in question was not large, I made a mental note to remember to increase my donation the following month to compensate.

An hour later, and just as I was wrapping up the paperwork, the issue of the tithing popped back into my head. I decided, quite out of the blue, to simply write the check for the donation right then while I was thinking about it and while there was still money left in the account, what with Christmas coming on and all. So I wrote the check and put it in my church papers to turn in on Sunday, got my elk hunting clothes on, and started the pickup.

With just a couple hours of daylight left I decided to check out a place I had found the previous spring while bear hunting in upper Willow Creek, which basically amounted to a few little conjoined meadows splattered on the steep face of a timbered mountain. There had been plenty of elk sign there during the spring green-up, but I had never hunted there in the fall and wasn't sure what to expect. If nothing else, I knew I could get up there before dark and it was a change of scenery and it might give me some clues for planning the weekend.

I parked at a bend in the Forest Service road in the mouth of the canyon and hoofed it up to the parks. A trickle of sweat dribbled down my back as I settled in under a little pine tree that gave me a good view of the park below and the hillside across. About forty-five minutes of hunting time remained of the day and I was unusually content to sit under that tree the whole time, soaking up the quiet and breathing the crisp mountain air.

Just before dark about 20 elk filed out of the timber and into the meadow below me and I killed a spike bull, legal in those days, with a slam-dunk 75 yard shot. I gutted him out by flashlight and pulled him up on some deadfall for retrieval the next day, and the whole time I couldn't quit thinking that the spike bull at my feet and the tithing check at home in my church papers were connected by a lot more than mere coincidence.

*****

"Any bulls?" my daughter Jessica asked.

I propped the binoculars out and methodically scanned the line of elk traipsing towards us.

"None close that I can see," I whispered. "Just get ready and shoot that cow coming along the fence."

The early dawn was just breaking and we had bellied up on a slab of a little rockpile, intercepting a big herd of elk that were making their way onto a private ranch from feeding during the night in some hay fields far below.

"Are you sure there aren't any bulls? Jessi calmly asked again.

"Man alive," I hissed, somewhat annoyed. "No. I don't see any bulls. You have never killed an elk. Just shoot that cow and do it now."

Jessi was just 13 years old, and in her second year of hunting. She had killed a nice whitetail buck her first year, but she never did get a chance at an elk that season. She told me several times before the season started that she would only shoot a buck that was bigger than the one she got last year. I didn't believe her. Using the past experiences with her older brothers and sister as a guide, I knew that the thirteen-year-olds in our family shoot first and measure later, but this was not the case with Jessi. During the first week of the season we had crept up on a scattered herd of about a dozen deer, and I spotted a decent basket-sized 3-point buck in the group.

"Hey Jessi," I whispered. "There's a buck."

Jessi craned her neck up and looked, scanning the deer with her eyes until she saw the buck. She looked at him for about a second, but made no move for the rifle slung over her shoulder.

"That's not bigger than last year's," she said, rolling her eyes like I had just wasted a bunch of her time, and wagged her head as if to say, "C'mon Dad, get with it."

So when she said on the way home that she also wanted to get a bull elk this year I had no choice but to believe her. Eventually she conceded that she might shoot a cow on her general tag if that was all that could be found. Montana allows youth hunters to shoot a legal bull or an antlerless elk on a general tag in most areas of the state, and as usual she already had the whole thing out sorted out.

I marveled at her calm, strong will. Jessi is the youngest of our four children and while pulling the trigger might be new to her, hunting certainly is not. I can remember her in a car seat dressed a in little home-made orange vest, gnawing on her bottle, gawking out the pickup window while we bounced up some Forest Service road. She was about six years old the year I quite miraculously killed a bull elk with Kim and her in tow. I gutted out the bull while she looked on in fascination. Seizing on a teaching moment, Kim asked Jessi where the elk's spirit went after Daddy killed it. Jessi furrowed her brow and quite innocently said, "Into the gut pile?"

Another time when Jessi was maybe 8 or 9, I had borrowed a meat grinder from my neighbor William to grind up some elk burger. The actual meat cutting took longer than expected and when I quit to go to bed I still had a couple of buckets of meat left. I got up about 6 o'clock in the morning and started grinding away in order to get the borrowed grinder returned on time. Jessi wandered into the kitchen in her pink flannel sleeper pajamas, her hair all blanket tousled, her eyes sleepy and blinking, her nose testing the air.

"Smells like meat, huh Dad," she said. "Smells good." Then she pulled up a stool and helped me grind and package the burger. And that is how Jessi grew up. Parents and older siblings made animals into venison, venison into white packages of freezer meat, and white packages of freezer meat into dinner. Now, finally, it was her turn.

A few days before the elk hunt Jessi had handed me a folded piece of notebook paper, pausing to make sure I was paying attention.

"I want to do this tomorrow," Jessi said.

I unfolded the paper and saw a stick figure drawing of a girl hunter shooting an impossibly big stick figure elk, and scrawled beneath in the distinct handwriting of her older brother Devin was the following note. "COUPON- Get out of school for one day to go hunting with Dad."

I took a moment to mentally review my upcoming work schedule.

"I can't tomorrow, but how about Friday?" I countered.

"Okay," Jessi shrugged, and she turned and disappeared down the hallway.

Devin had been away from home for over a year on a church mission. A voracious hunter himself, he had sacrificed all of last season and would miss this one too, and I could tangibly see the longing in that crude sketch. It dawned on me that this coupon was bigger than a stick figure sketch and a coupon to miss school. It was Devin's way of being a part of it however he could, and an expression of caring for his little sister. A momentary wave of regret hit me for putting it off until Friday. Why would you get in the way of something like that? Later that evening Jessi assured me that Friday would be OK, and so it was a date.

As dawn broke on the Thursday morning before the Friday hunt, I spotted a large herd of elk several miles away through my spotting scope. A lunch-hour investigation of the area indicated that the elk were crossing a little section of publicly accessible land before crossing onto the safety of the posted ranch. I told Jessi of my discovery that afternoon, and she shrugged confidently and asked me if I had seen any bulls.

Long before daylight the next morning Jessi and I made our way to the rock slab, the mewings and chirpings of many elk on the move coming from out of the gloom ahead of us. I was worried that the herd would be across the fence and onto the private ranch before shooting light and most of them were, but a few antlerless stragglers finally appeared along the fence and plodded into range. Jessi looked at me again. I glassed the string of elk again. I shook my head. No bulls.

Jessi matter-of-factly pushed the gun forward over my daypack and settled in for the shot, as if she has done this every day of her life. The closest cow on the fence line paused and the gun went off. The cow hunched and staggered. The gun went off again. A clean miss. Another shot, and this time the old cow collapsed. I looked over at Jessi and her face was all spread out in a smile as big as the Big Sky above us. Her very first elk, and she had shot it well.

We made our way over to the cow, took a bunch of pictures from a bunch of angles, and gutted her out. Then we headed for home to get Kim and the horses.

By one o'clock in the afternoon the elk was hanging in quarter bags in the meat cooler and Kim and Jessi had decided we should head up to Ovando for the evening deer hunt. By 4:00 in the afternoon we were taking pictures of Kim's 5-point whitetail buck, the biggest she had ever killed. Since both Kim and Jessi had also drawn A-9 elk tags for the area, which are a second tag good only for cow elk, we thought we should just burn up the rest of the hunting day by driving around and glassing and then head over to Trixi's Antler Saloon and Restaurant for dinner to celebrate our great day.

Just before dark, and way out in the middle of some rolling sagebrush hills, I spotted 8 or 9 cow elk. They were a long ways away, a couple of miles at least, but I thought I knew whose land they were on and how to get a little closer. We hopped back in the truck and drove over to the ranch yard, got permission from the landowner, and took off in a direct line toward the elk. We had maybe 20 minutes of daylight left. Maybe. We didn't have enough time for any pussy-footing or a long and fancy stalk. I felt that we had no choice but to walk right at them, and the terrain and the wind and the remaining light all blended together like magic. My eyes simply could not believe what they were seeing when Jessi set her gun barrel over the shooting sticks and aimed it at a big, mature cow elk grazing undisturbed 75 yards away. Three shots later and her second cow elk of the day dropped. Her second legally killed elk! On the same day! She's 13 years old!

We filed into Trixi's for dinner about 9 o'clock with bloody sleeves and bloody pants and great big smiles. By then my belly was really empty and my back was really sore and my knife was really dull, but I was completely awestruck about our most excellent day. Two girls. Two cow elk and one big buck. One great day. We all ate expensive steaks and told whoever would listen about our hunt, and I couldn't believe the story myself even as I was telling it.

A few miles into the drive home, Kim and Jessi's eyes shut and their heads slouched against the head rests. I kept the radio off and let them sleep, my mind wandering in little smiley faces about the nearly impossible events of the day.

Eventually, my thoughts turned to Devin. I thought of him far away from home, dressed in a suit and tie, working as a missionary, completely missing this hunting season. I pictured him in some little apartment a few weeks ago, taking both the thought and the time out of a busy day to scratch out those stick figures and a little coupon for Jessi to get out of school for a day to go hunting with Dad. And today was that day.

*What are the odds?*

Such a simple, little, and forgettable act of kindness that somehow lead to such a fantastic, magnificent, and unforgettable day. I marveled at so much good coming from so little goodness, as usual, and I simply could not bring myself to dismiss the events of the day and the power of that little coupon as merely a fluke of random chance.

*No, really- What are the odds?*

What are the odds of taking a 13 year old girl out of school for one day during the middle of general rifle season and she kills two elk- one in the morning and one in the evening? And not just two elk- her very first two elk? What are the odds of having Kim add her biggest whitetail buck on top of all that? And what are the odds that all of this occurred on the exact day when Jessi used a coupon from her older brother, far away from home serving a church mission?

I have been at this long enough to know that like life, sometimes hunting isn't about the odds. Sometimes, very rarely, experiences transcend statistics and probabilities and plops us right smack-dab into the impossible. Days when we recognize that divine powers are mercifully directing traffic, lining up the stars just so over our unknowing heads, connecting all those otherwise unconnectable dots for us. Days when we are, or should be, quite bluntly reminded that the universe is a very big and mysterious place.

And somehow and for some reason, on that very day, I had participated as all these unconnectable dots had miraculously connected. As the reach of the headlights fade to black beneath the star filled night, I am indeed once again reminded that the universe is a very big and mysterious place.

# ALMOST THERE

*"But the wisdom that is from above is first pure,*
*then peaceable, gentle, and easy to be intreated,*
*full of mercy and good fruits" James 3:17*

The cool grass felt good on the bottoms of my fevered feet. I shuffled across the backyard and eased myself up onto the kid's trampoline. Clenching my teeth against the pounding headache, I situated my pillow and lay on my back, spread-eagled, looking up into the stars, soaking up the chill off the mat. The mid-July night was dark and clear, and a swirl of breeze cooled the damp sweat on my forehead.

I was sick. I was very sick. I had viral spinal meningitis. Two weeks worth so far and no end in sight. Two solid weeks of puking up everything but Ritz Crackers and Sprite. Two weeks of Percoset tablets just to take a bit of the edge off the headache so I could get a few hours of sleep. Two weeks of lying flat on my back with my head wedged between two pillows. Two full weeks of golden summer wasted. Two weeks and still the fever and chills and nausea and crushing headache refused to relent. I had never, ever, never in my life been this sick for this long and my nerves were shot and my patience gone and my system completely exhausted. At the moment I was all fevered up, and even though it was late, it sounded good to get outside for some fresh, cool air.

Back on the afternoon of July 3rd, the day before Kim's extended family were to begin arriving at our house for a family reunion, I got unusually droopy driving home from work in Missoula. When I got home, I tried for the better part of an hour to set up a big wall tent that I'd borrowed for the reunion. After the wind blew it over for the second time and the falling tent frame dug a nasty gash in my shin, I uncharacteristically lost my cool and stormed inside the house. As I tromped down the hall, Kim called over her shoulder from the kitchen and reminded me that we'd been invited by our mechanic up in Lincoln, who moonlights as the lead singer of a local band, to a dance that night at Trixi's up in Ovando. I blew it off, and told Kim that I didn't feel too well and that I needed to get to bed. She was visibly disappointed, but I went in and doctored up my shin and crawled into bed anyway, sure that I had simply hit the wall and that with a little extra sleep I'd get feeling better.

That night I came down with the classic 24-hour flu symptoms of fever-chills-fever, and as the house filled with relatives the next day, a crushing and relentless headache added into the mix. I threw Advil at it. Aspirin. Tylenol. I took twice the maximum dose of whatever we had but still could not dent that headache. Finally, after two days and no relief, I relented and Kim drove me into Now Care in Missoula.

Reclined on the passenger seat of my pickup on the way to the doctor, my head sandwiched between two pillows, I tried to lighten the somber mood some and said to Kim, "If this turns out bad for me, remind me to tell you where my cash-stash is."

She turned her face away like she does when the tears come up, and when she looked back at me the fear in her eyes jolted me into thinking that now my little joke had the potential for the bitterest of irony.

We got to the clinic and the entrance paperwork asked for the name of my doctor. I don't have a doctor. I don't go to the doctor. I don't like doctors and their self-inflated air of godliness and the uncanny way they have of talking down to you. Besides, I don't have time to be sick, and when I do get to feeling poorly I prefer to nurse it better myself. But this felt major, and I sincerely thought that maybe a tumor in my brain had ruptured or something of the like.

The doctor, a slender and energetic young guy who I found myself liking anyway, finally came into the room and efficiently took a couple of vials of blood for some tests. He told us that the overwhelming likelihood was that I had some odd virus and that in another day or two it should work itself out. He actually said that he might suspect meningitis but that I didn't seem sick enough to have meningitis. If I wasn't coming around and feeling better in another couple of days, or if I got to feeling worse, I should come back. He'd call me in two days with the results of the blood tests, and with that he bustled out the door.

Back home at the reunion, I made a few attempts to get out of bed and mingle a little, but every time I spent fifteen minutes on my feet the headache would kick into overdrive and the nausea would return and I'd shuffle back to bed. Once, when Kim opened the door to the bedroom to check on me, the simple smell of dinner cooking turned my stomach over and made me wretch. Kim was wearing herself out trying to host the reunion by herself and also take care of me, and she commented a couple times that she was sure glad that she didn't make me take her to the dance in Ovando that first night.

Two days later and I was most assuredly not feeling any better. Late that night I found myself back at Now Care, sitting on a hospital bed in a darkened room with double fluid IVs dripping into my arms. The blood tests had confirmed that my white count was up, but that was as much as they knew for sure. If a flush of fluid into my bloodstream made me feel better then they would know that the diluted virus was in my bloodstream. It did not make me feel any better. Meningitis now became a better bet, and a young lady doctor had me pop a Valium and gave me a local anesthetic to prep me for a spinal tap. She had me lay on my side in one of those horrible hospital gowns, thumbing along my lower spine for a few seconds, and then she'd poke the needle in my back. Then she'd say "nope" and try again, and she must have poked my back six or seven times, remarking more than once how "thick" the area was. Finally she got the needle between two vertebrae.

"Uh-oh," she said. "I don't believe it. The needle's too short."

I heard the voice of a nurse behind her ask how long the needle was.

"Two and a half inches," the doctor replied.

"Well, doc," I said through the Valium fog. "You should know by now that you can't hit the sweet spot with only two and a half inches."

A tense, unsure laughter speckled the room and Kim asked that they put me completely under.

Thirty minutes later a different doctor, the husband of the lady doctor, sat me up and crunched me forward and hit the spinal fluid on his first try. At one o'clock in the morning we knew for sure. Viral spinal meningitis. The good news was that there are rarely any long term problems after recovery from viral meningitis and that it most likely was not contagious. The bad news was that they could only treat the symptoms until the virus worked itself out of my system, normally in four to six weeks.

"How much do you weigh?" the lady doctor asked as she scribbled on a prescription pad.

"About 235," I said.

"OK. You can take one of these Percoset. If it doesn't help, you can try two. Never take more than two or you are likely to start seeing dragons coming out of the curtains. Got it?"

"Yes Ma'am."

I was given the option of going home or checking into the hospital where they could offer me a little better pain management for about $3,000.00 a day. Kim checked me into a $65.00 motel instead, and early in the morning she left for home to send the relatives off from the reunion. That was ten days ago. Ten long and brutal days ago.

The gentle bounce of getting up on the trampoline faded. I shut my eyes and let the breeze cool me, but when I closed my eyes the inside of my head started spinning in big, slow-moving circles and crazy splashes of orange and red kaleidoscoped across my mind's eye. I knew it wasn't because of the Percoset. I didn't like the loss of control, the nausea, or the freaky dreams the medicine gave me so I took it only as a last resort and hadn't had any since the night before. I opened up my eyes and stared into space. Somehow the view of the night sky above me steadied my wobbly head. I lay like that for a long time, maybe an hour, completely motionless and quiet, soaking up the chill from the mat, looking into the deep stars.

Without warning, great tears welled up in my eyes and rolled off my face onto my pillow. I wasn't really crying, and these were not the tears of sadness or anger or fear, and they did not come because of sickness or exhaustion or pain, or because all of these had combined and I had finally hit the wall. No, not because I had hit the wall but rather because I had somehow broken through the wall and beyond it into a new place, a place peaceful and immense and serene. I became distinctly aware of the pattern of my own heartbeat and measured the methodical rise and fall of my breath, marveling in all of it. My senses heightened and connected in a remarkable way, hard to explain, and I felt a new intensity in the breeze on my face. I could feel the breeze wanting to drift me up and away from the trampoline and into the place where the wind goes. I almost tangibly imagined myself floating away from my body and into the stars. The sum of all existence shrunk until all that was left was me and the breeze and the stars. I relaxed and loosed myself, trying to let go, teeter-tottering for several moments in the dimensions between the spiritual and the physical. Between the conscious and unconscious. Somewhere between gravity and weightlessness.

I lay like that, suspended and enraptured, until the door to the back deck opened and Kim hollered my name. I did not answer. The wet tears still clung to my face and the healing air in the breeze continued to caress me in beauty. For a while I troubled over my state of mind, conflicted about whether my sickness-weakened state was the cause of this experience or merely the preparation for it. Whether this qualified as revelation or institutionalization. I decided that it did not matter. Either way it was absolutely happening, right here in my backyard, lying still on the kids' trampoline, looking up into the stars.

For the next several minutes an undeniable spiritual wellness spread over me like freshly thrown flannel sheets, true and real and pure as the Montana air. Drifting along in the night sky, the canopy of stars seemed to contract to mere specks of light and then expand into an infinite universe and then contract to mere specks again. I sensed with positive surety that somewhere out there in the cosmos there is somebody who knows me by name and knows that I am this very minute in the backyard, lying on my trampoline, suffering from spinal meningitis. That there are beings out there somewhere who know the fears and hear the prayers of my good wife inside the house. And that there are many. Maybe even infinite. Maybe they are never-ending generations, both past and future, like a pedigree chart going both directions forever, and for an awkward moment or two I contemplated this little glimpse of eternity, the conception of angels and spirits and people all merging into one. The tears continued to seep, and immersed as I was in The Big Picture, the thought came clearly to me that we must certainly underestimate the volume of existence in our sphere. Intelligence. Consciousness. Energy. Life. Surely there is life in the expanding and contracting of the lights in the universe over my head. Certainly there is life in the virus that infects my spinal fluid. Surely there is life in the grass that cooled my feet. Without question there is life in the dirt that grows the grass that cooled my feet. Life in the warming core of the earth. Life in the stars. Glorious and Infinite life in the Sun, and surely the breeze on my face is the literal breathing of the earth.

The door on the back deck opened again, and this time an urgency sounded in Kim's voice. I called back, and after a minute or two sat up slow and easy. Almost instantly the pounding headache returned. The life went completely out of the breeze and I could feel the chills coming on. I scooted off the trampoline, and the grass seemed much colder as I tip-toed across the lawn and into the house and back into bed.

Kim creaked the door open to the bedroom and asked if I needed anything. She pestered me with a few questions about being outside, but my answers were simple and vague. A sincere concern furrowed her brow, and she shut the door softly and left the room, leaving me alone. I buried my head under the pillows. The returning headache and chills depleted what remained of my fragile will, emptying me, leaving me utterly deflated and hollow. A fresh wave of exhaustion and headache crashed over me with crushing force. Fresh, new tears came up, but these were now the tears of an intense and unexplainable loneliness and melancholy.

*Am I the only one? Am I the only one who knows?*

Something truly meaningful had just happened, that was for sure, but I do not know exactly what and even less exactly why. With no reserve and so little fortitude left, all I knew for sure right then was this. I almost saw it. I was almost there. Almost into the stars. Almost to the place where the breathing of the wind goes, and the very last thing I wanted right then was to be misunderstood.

# WIND

*"The wind bloweth where it listeth, and thou hearest the sound thereof, but canst not tell whence it cometh, and whither it goeth: so is every one that is born of the Spirit" John 3:8*

The wind was all wrong, right at our backs. Even so, my eager young sons Jacob and Devin had convinced me that this was the place. The elk would come. They had seen it with their own eyes twice in the week before archery season opened. All we had to do was set up by the spot where the fence sagged and they would come. When I first stood at the broken spot in the fence, seeing the spiderweb of freshly worn elk trails funneling from the brush into this exact spot, I had to admit that I thought they were right. The elk would come, or at least they had been coming through here recently and regularly. I knelt in the dust and fingertipped one of the dozens of tracks that pocked the landing. Nice and fresh. Evidently, the elk were spending their days bedded in the security of the posted river bottom and their nights feeding in the hay fields behind us. I nodded with approval toward my anxious young bowhunters. This was a good place to set up, that was for sure, but we still had to deal with the wind.

A majority of the trails meandered in from slightly north, so if we set up a few yards south of the crossing the wind might be sideways of the elk when they came in. Not ideal, but not bad either, and so we got to work and roughed out a ground blind. I paced the distance from the crossing back to the blind. Twenty eight yards. Perfect. We knelt in turn and practiced drawing our bows toward the crossing. Every few minutes I'd stand and scan the brush beyond with my binoculars, but it was a little early yet. We'd have to wait.

As the shadows from the cottonwoods lengthened, I hoped that the evening wind at our backs might quiet some. Quite often in this part of Montana during the late summer and early fall you wake up to chilly, calm mornings and eat lunch to a bit of a westerly breeze. By late afternoon, the wind gusts up some and blows the grass clippings off the sidewalk. Evenings are the wild card. Sometimes, as the sun sets, it is so windless and calm outside that it feels like the inside of a church. Other evenings the curtains in the bedroom flap back and forth and you have to get up and shut the window just to get to sleep. That's how it felt tonight, like it was going to be a close-the-window-to-get-to-sleep night. And blowing right at our backs.

I glanced over at Devin and Jacob. They couldn't care less about the wind. In all likelihood, they didn't even know to be worried about it. They twiddled about, fussing over their bows and picking at the grass. Their whole world right now was the impatient anticipation of an elk walking up to that broken wire and jumping the fence, drawing their bows, and sending their arrows into its heart. I'd seen more improbable things happen out elk hunting, but then again I'd seen lots of probable things not happen too. We'd just have to wait and see.

Nothing about the wind had changed much when my binoculars showed me an elk way in the distance, maybe a mile away, and just for a second as it moved between a couple of patches of brush. I clicked my teeth to get the boys' attention and pointed. They immediately tensed into shooting position, wide-eyed, their hands flexing on the grips of their bows, eyebrows up, pointing back and forth in hunter's sign language. A few minutes later a herd of about thirty elk were roping out of the brush five or six hundred yards away, heading right for us, but the angle was all wrong.

"We're toast," I whispered, and set my bow back in the grass.

Devin shot me a perturbed glance, clearly annoyed. Jacob flexed his grip on his bow and stayed riveted on the elk, which plodded into the open and started grazing towards us on the walk. Right at us. Right into our wind.

At about 250 yards, a cow elk jerked her head up. The whole herd came to attention, noses in the air, ears wide and alert. The lead cow turned in a tight circle and stopped, nose into our wind again. The elk wheeled all at the same time and crashed off, and a scant few seconds later we heard them splash across the river a half a mile away.

I expected to see a couple of long, sad faces when I lowered my binoculars. Their faces were long all right, but it was because they were slack-jawed with amazement.

"No way," one of them said.

We gathered up our gear and walked across the hay field by moonlight. We talked about elk and their incredible noses and I told the boys that if they would be patient and wait until the time was right, wait for a day when there was a north or an east wind, that they stood a real good chance of getting a shot at an elk at that spot.

The short drive home was unusually quiet, each of us lost in our thoughts, and when I looked at my young and inexperienced sons I hoped they had the capacity to know that virtually nothing could make them more successful hunters, or more successful men for that matter, than to really understand what they had just seen.

*****

A faint smear of orange painted the eastern skyline as I edged up over the little rise and eased around the Altar. I brushed the snow out of my sitting spot and settled in, slipping out of my daypack, chambering a cartridge in my rifle, and wiping the sweat off my forehead with my sleeve. The past hour had been spent in the dark scrabbling up the steep scree face to the south to get up here and keep the west wind in my favor. When Dave first showed me this spot we had parked at the bottom, right in the mouth of the draw, and hiked up the hill with the breeze at our back with only a patch of trees for cover. The next time I hunted here I was by myself, and halfway up the hill I spotted a one-horned five-point bull elk bedded with a spike in a little stringer of pines just below the ridge. Below the ridge, and right in my wind. Despite my best maneuverings, all I ended up with on that day was a momentary look at the two bulls skylined another ridge away as they moved out. Thereafter, despite the extra effort, I always hiked up the scree face.

The wind blew firm into my face and chilled the wet hair under the brim of my hat. Given the conditions, I had chosen wisely. I propped out my binoculars and started to scan, but shooting light was still several minutes away. I leaned back into the Altar, fighting off the chills. The Altar is the name I gave a pile of shale rocks about six foot square and four feet tall that is situated at a slight knoll where two nice timbered draws come together. From here I can shoot to either canyon and have a good view of an open sagebrush park above me as well. The Altar had obviously been arranged by somebody for some reason at some time long past, and of course I have no idea who or why or when. Due to its location, my best guess is a hunter built it but I can't imagine a hunter with that much extra energy. At any rate, the Altar can be a good bet for the first couple hours of the morning, especially late in the season when there is weather. A few years before, I took up the track of big, black-horned mule deer buck in a fresh skiff of snow early one morning, and he still ranks as one of the biggest bucks I've ever killed. A year or two later, I snapped a picture of my wife Kim and the nice four-point buck she shot from the Altar that ended up being printed in the Fishing and Hunting News. Another morning I spotted a wall-hanger six-point bull elk all by himself in the upper park right at daylight and completely botched it, and this at a time when I was experienced enough to have done much better.

Shooting light came and went and it became evident that there wouldn't be any wall-hanger bulls or pictures for the Fishing and Hunting News this morning. All I could find were a couple of muley does at the edge of the timber. I hung in there, resisting my ever-present urge to see the other side of the mountain, at least for a few more minutes. The gusty wind rippled the sage, still blowing perfect, when all of a sudden I saw the tip of a deer antler wobble directly below me about forty yards away. A smallish three-point mule deer buck gradually appeared, nipping at this bush and that, feeding right towards me. He had obviously been below me, obscured from my view earlier by the curve of the hill. I froze. He kept coming, oblivious. I wasn't interested in making so small a buck into venison jerky this early in the season, but without any other options I was interested in seeing how close he would come. Thirty yards.... twenty yards....fifteen. I tried to avoid eye contact but at a mere ten yards he finally swiveled his head sideways, quizzical like, and looked right at me. His body braced to attention and he jumped sideways. I thought it was over right there, but he stopped after that one jump and kept staring right at me. Right through me. I could see his nostrils flaring wide, but the wind continued firm into my face. He'd dip his head low and yank it up, stomping his front foot. He seemed to know something was wrong but his nose couldn't tell him what. Over the next minute or so he actually ducked and bobbed several yards closer, nearly into spitting distance.

After a bit, the little buck moseyed stiff-legged around to my right, crossed the ridge, and circled around below me, still a scant twenty yards away but now moving directly toward my scent.

*Five....four....three....two...*

Shale clattered as the deer suddenly blew and exploded downhill, gobbling up the hillside in thirty foot bounds. By the time I got to my feet and turned around, the buck was across the bottom and running full out along a game trail up the other side of the draw and in seconds disappeared over the far ridge. I stretched my cramped muscles and grinned, pacing off the closest track at seven yards, and I thought that all too often in life the only difference between being stupid and smart, between aware and unaware, of being able or being unable, is in which way the wind is blowing.


*****


I followed when the tail-lights of Brian's pickup left the dirt road, paralleled an old range fence in a patch of sagebrush, and blinked off. He grabbed out his gun and daypack, locked the doors, and pocketed his keys. Stars still speckled the crisp November morning sky and we had the heater on full blast in my old International Scout. Brian creaked the door open and piled in with Dave and me. Our plan was to leave Brian's truck at the bottom of a long and sloping canyon, drive to the top and work our way down, hunting the four or five miles of bumps and draws along the way for a bull elk or a big mule deer buck.

The morning dawned brilliant blue and there was a little fluff of snow on top. Conditions were perfect, and our hopes inflated even further when a herd of a dozen cow elk trotted out of the trees and crossed right below us as we were parking the Scout.

About nine o'clock, Brian's wanderlust got the best of him and he decided to drop off and hunt the next canyon over, thinking he had a better chance of seeing an elk with antlers  over        there. Dave and I had never been to this place before and it had been dark when we drove up. Knowing that it would most likely be dark by the time we got out, we were a little concerned about finding his truck.

"It's easy," Brian said. "Once the ridge peters out on the flat, just bear to the right until you hit the fence. Follow the fence until you get to the truck. Piece of cake." And with that he turned and disappeared into the trees.

Dave and I enjoyed a fabulous morning of hunting, seeing another herd of cow elk and well over a hundred deer, including about twenty-five mule deer bucks that ranged from small to medium. We passed them all up looking for a big boy. It seemed like the animals were up and feeding everywhere, even after the sun was fully up, and we spent most of the day behind the binoculars watching game.

I figured we were a shade over halfway down the canyon at about 4:00 in the afternoon when the westerly wind went noticeably calm and the air warmed slightly. Directly to the north, I noticed that the whole sky, top to bottom, had turned the color of steel wool. As evening began to settle in, we could see the frost colored haze of snow showers coming at us with the blackening sky, but we figured we still had plenty of time to get out before the snow showers hit us.

In the next forty minutes the temperature dropped at least thirty degrees and the wind picked up and straightened out, directly out of the north. Before we knew it the steel wool sky boiled over us, and I got worried for the first time when Dave said out loud that we might be in some trouble.

The storm hit us like a snowy fist. The snow blasted in a whiteout, horizontally, and the temperature crashed to below zero. The arctic wind blew with hatred and vengeance and anger, and it seemed perfectly natural to consider the storm as a real and living threat. Mean and dark and unpredictable, like a bad drunk, and I now understand better why hurricanes are given human names. Dave and I dropped off the ridge top and huddled in a little stand of Christmas trees, putting on every extra piece of clothing we had. The wind and snow and accompanying darkness were so fierce that I literally could not completely see trees twenty yards in front of my face, and at times it became difficult to tell if we were still going downhill. Whenever we faced a decision about which way to go, we always bore to the right, literally praying that we would find that fence.

I had on a pair of rag wool gloves that were wet from the days hunt, and in minutes my hands were freezing cold. I alternated putting one hand in a pocket and then the other, well aware that these are the kinds of storms that rescue workers recover bodies from three days later. For the moment my feet and body were okay, although I doubted if we could survive the night out in the open if the storm continued. I wasn't particularly terrified, although the tension was building for sure, but I did feel particularly small and vulnerable, convinced that this storm would just as soon kill me as not and that she did not have one ounce of mercy for the fact that I am married to a good woman who loves me and have four small kids at home who still need me.

We kept moving, downhill and to the right we hoped, and Dave shouted above the wind that he thought we had been on the flat for a while. I agreed. We banked a hard right, or at least what we guessed was a hard right. By now darkness had overtaken us and the storm had picked up in fury. We leaned into the wind and snow, unable to see anything meaningful, neither of us saying what both of us were thinking, which was that if we didn't find that fence it could be lights out for both of us. The drama was short-lived, however, because in about five minutes we hit the fence and shortly after that a pair of hazy headlights bumped into view. We piled in the truck and Brian, whose face showed considerable relief, wheeled the truck in an arc through the sage and back to the fence.

"Let's get the hell out of here," Dave said.

Within a few hundred yards, the inbound truck tracks in the snow were already blown out. I peeled the partially frozen gloves off my hands and threw them on the dashboard, rubbing my hands together in front of the heater vent. Both hands went severe pins-and-needles before normal feeling returned, and by then we had heard that Brian had taken one look at the darkening sky and high-tailed it off his side of the canyon and had actually come down our ridge looking for us. He missed us somehow, but figured by then that we'd already be back at the truck. We obviously weren't, and the later and colder and more ferocious the storm became, the more worried he got. He had been up and down that fence line for the past hour, wondering if or when he should go in to town to get help and call our wives, and what on earth he might say to them.

We spent the night in my camp trailer with the furnace on high and every propane burner lit. The storm blew itself out overnight but left a week's worth of bitter arctic air in its wake. The next morning the air temperature was close to twenty below zero, and the harsh reality of what yesterday might been didn't really hit me until I creaked the door open to Brian's truck and found my wool gloves frozen solid to the dashboard.

*****

The alarm clock went off and I almost stayed in bed when I heard the wind howling through the chimney. I got up anyway, as much to avoid a day of honey-do's as anything. Besides, sometimes the wind up in the mountains is different than here at the house, especially down off the ridges in the dark timber.

By the time the sun was up I'd made it to the top of the mountain. The wind wasn't any different here. If anything, it had picked up some extra steam. The tops of the big fir trees swayed and swished, back and forth, slow dancing with the gusting wind, and lower to the ground the frost-killed aspen leaves fluttered off the limb ends and skittered across the forest floor. Dry grasses rolled in waves across the open parks. Big white-and-gray clouds, the kind that you can imagine into animal shapes, paraded across the sky. As if the wind had given it a list of chores to do, the whole world seemed busy and active, pulsing and breathing and alive.

I dropped off a ridge with the wind in my face and, following a series of game trails, worked down into the thicker timber. Even in the trees, the forest was full of motion and noise, difficult hunting conditions to say the least. After a few hours of fruitless search my patience wore thin, and I cursed the dirty, rotten wind. When I stopped for a sandwich and a soda, the thought came that this might have been a good day after all to spend catching up on some household chores, so I gathered my gear and at the next fork in the game trail angled back up toward the ridge.

I poked along up the trail, remembering an old logging road that I would soon have to cross and thinking about that road reminded me of one more little draw I should check out when right in front of me, as in *ten yards* in front of me, a nice, mature 4-point whitetail buck lay in his bed. *Asleep* in his bed! As in *asleep with his eyes closed*!

I froze, dumbfounded, my mind unable to process the view my eyes were giving it. The dirty, rotten wind had carried my scent away from the buck and the dirty, rotten wind had covered the noise of my footfalls and I had simply walked up to within ten yards of a mature whitetail buck without even waking it up which, of course, is impossible. Absolutely not possible. My mind flashed the thought that the deer was dead, but his head was up, so he wasn't dead. Surely he must be wounded. Maybe he had been hit by an errant arrow during bow season or maybe he collided with a car down.....

The buck's eyes bolted open and in the same motion he came six feet out of his bed and in two jumps disappeared out of view. Only then, way too late, did I think of the rifle dangling off my shoulder.

*****

When the bottom of the sun hit the top of the skyline, I stood up in my treestand and stretched. The hot September afternoon had gradually smoldered into evening, and in another half hour it would be the hunter's half hour. My bow hung from a hook screwed into a limb of the cottonwood tree to my left, arrow nocked and at the ready, but I had not disturbed the bow in the two hours since I hung it there. The animals weren't moving much in the hot, still weather.

I took the little squeeze bottle of talc out of my pocket and shook it, puffing some dust into the air to check the direction of the wind. The talc smoke wafted and rolled lazily upward, dissipating into the leaves above me. Not much wind. None really. From ten feet up in the tree I should be fine.

After twenty minutes I sat back down on the little foam covered seat of the treestand, shifting my weight every few minutes, impatiently scanning the hay field and river brush every minute or two with my binoculars. Finally, two whitetail does appeared behind me at the edge of the river bottom, angling roughly in my direction. Glad for any action at all, I stood up and situated my feet, glassing the deer. I had a whitetail doe tag in my daypack, but this whole ritual was entirely premature since having these distant deer end up within bow range would depend entirely on a liberal dose of good luck. I shook the talc again and again it drifted straight up. Very good. The deer seemed to be in no hurry, nibbling their way along the edge of the brush. Fifteen minutes later they picked their heads up and plodded up the exact trail that would put them broadside and just eighteen yards from my stand. I grinned and eased my bow off the hook, and just as I did I felt a brush of warm air on my neck. Great. No wind for three hours and now, just as a couple of does start up the slam-dunk trail, a breeze starts up and blows right at them.

The deer were still coming however. Maybe the warm air lifted over them or something, but they still seemed perfectly unaware. The little breeze continued to drift at my neck and the deer kept coming up the trail. I stayed focused and still, just in case, but I doubted it would last much longer. Sure enough, about seventy yards out one of the does stopped and wheezed, and they both whirled and high-stepped back into the thickets, their white tails swaggering back and forth. I shook my head and slumped my shoulders, blowing a disgusted puff of air between my teeth.

*Bad luck that…*

But I had scarcely put my bow on the hook and settled back into my seat when I heard several large ker-splashes in the river, again from behind me but this time to the south and out of my wind. Some elk were coming. I plucked the bow off the hook and situated my feet again.

*Yeah, buddy.*

This was going to work out better after all as I also had an elk tag in my daypack and, given the choice, I'd way rather hang a tag on a bull elk than a whitetail doe. I had to breathe deeply to control the surge of anticipation that waved over me, and I actually thought in my mind how lucky I was that the little breeze had come up and spooked off those does. Over the next several minutes, I could hear the cow elk calling and mewing behind me a couple of hundred yards back in the brush, and they were moving uncharacteristically south to north. With growing concern, I puffed some more talc into the breeze and you couldn't draw a straighter line from me to where the elk were heading. The wind at the back of my neck cooled slightly and drifted a little stronger and the elk crashed off before I even got to see them.

I looked up into the sky, half expecting to see a frowning face looking back at me, wagging a disapproving finger from the clouds.

*Oh, come on!*

Several deer appeared in the hay field from a quarter mile north, but nothing else showed itself on my trail. And then, as if adding insult to injury, just before I climbed out of my stand the breeze cooled dramatically and swapped ends, now blowing 180 degrees opposite and perfect into my treestand, but way too late to do any good. I lowered my bow out of the tree, gathered up my gear, and stomped back to the truck, downright offended.

*****

A dim thunder rumbled, distant and faint and out of place in the placid summer air, and when I looked up into the baby blue sky not a cloud could be seen. A few minutes later we heard the thunder again, maybe a little stronger, and directly west of us. A massive and ragged granite peak, nearly at eye level, blocked our view westward and offered no other clues. Besides that, it was nearly dinner time so we reeled up our fishing poles and headed back for the tent, mouths watering at the anticipation of some instant mashed potatoes cooked over the single propane burner.

Earlier that year, funds were a little scarcer than normal so I had talked Kim into a backpacking trek into the Beartooth Mountains of Montana for our summer trip. I'd been up here a couple of years before with a Boy Scout group, and the brutal majesty of those mountains was something I wanted Kim to see. So just before the first week of August we bought a $49.95 dome tent at Costco, dropped the kids off at Grandma's house for a week, and drove to the trailhead just out of Cooke City.

The first three or four miles of the trail are fairly gentle and serene, pleasant even, meandering past Lady of the Lake Lake and grassy meadows filled with wildflowers and willow-lined creeks that spill freestone over colorful cobble rocks and other such niceties. Then, after we'd had a little lunch break, I made a right hand turn on a faint trail, crossed a little creek on a fallen log, and pointed sharply uphill at a trail that disappeared into a nearly vertical chute, steep and rocky and narrow.

"You've got to be kidding," was all Kim said.

The next couple hours of hiking were like changing planets, and we climbed above the pines and meadows and freestone creeks and into a world of jagged granite and snow and sky. At the far side of Aero Lake, Kim went to work on some food while I pushed those lame little aluminum tent pegs into the shallow alpine soil at a steep angle and pitched the tent. We camped on the lee side of an abrupt rock ledge at almost 10,000 feet, well above timberline, and within a stone's throw of the lake. The brutal immensity of the place simply cannot be adequately described. This rugged country is just so close to the bone. Up here the rocks are harder, the water colder, the sky bluer, the food better tasting, and Kim said without hesitation that it was well worth the hike. The next afternoon we scrabbled boulder to boulder across a rockslide and showered in a little streak of water falling off the mountain. Late the next day, we heard the thunder as we fished in the creek between the two lakes for cutthroat trout.

When we got back to camp, the edges of the sky above the granite were nearly black and rolls of far-off thunder groaned almost non-stop. Strikes of lightning beyond the granite peaks flashed in the roiling sky. By the time Kim got back from the lake with a cook pot of water, the wind was gusting in swirls and the thunder was getting closer. Much closer, so I hastily put a couple of rocks on the tarp covering the backpacks and crawled into the tent. Kim wriggled into her sleeping bag. I unzipped a little window inside the tent, gawking into the oncoming storm. I actually heard it coming before it hit full force. At first I couldn't place the sound, something like a jet engine from a large airplane only lower in pitch, and when I finally realized what it was I looked down at Kim and said, "hang on."

Out of nowhere, a brilliant gash of lightning lit up the sky and exactly at the same instant a blast of thunder cracked and boomed, rolling off the mountains for several seconds. The wind racked across us in violent waves, pummeling our little tent, and what I remember most is squatting up in the tent, splay legged, hands wide, supporting the small dome, watching with growing alarm out of the net window as the fiberglass poles of the tent bent and curved and waffled like four-weight flyrods. The rain fly would lift way up and then a corner would catch the wind and slam it back down. Kim buried her head into her sleeping bag and shut her eyes. Another simultaneous lightning strike and wicked crack of thunder, but this time sheets of rain blowing sideways slammed into us with the wind, spattering against the fabric with such power that I truly didn't think our new little tent was going to make it.

Unbelievable strikes of lightning and thunder constantly rocked the sky, and I was gripped in a genuine and cowering fear. Fear of that one lightning flash blasting into our tent and our screams and the smell of scorched hair and our dead bodies discovered by other hikers two days from now. Fear of the storm ripping the tent right out of my hands and an avalanche slide of boulders tumbling off the granite mountain, crushing and mangling us to powder. Worse yet, fear of that lightning strike taking only Kim, leaving me all alone in the world with the four kids back at Grandma's house to raise by myself. I deflected the thoughts and channeled as much energy as I could into steadying the little tent.

*Hang on - come on little guy. Whoa-whoa! Come on, hang on.*

For fifteen or twenty minutes the storm slashed at us. With considerable relief, I finally noticed the winds begin to peter out and the thunder and lightning drifting farther and farther east. After another five minutes the wind downshifted once more, to a swirling breeze, and then once more and into neutral. Kim opened her eyes and asked if it was over. Yes, it was over. At least for now.

We crawled out of the tent, surprised that the setting sun was already peaceful and warm on our faces, and that the big sky to the west was completely blue and bright and overwhelming again. The black clouds and thunder growled farther and farther away and, twenty minutes later, were completely out of sight.

Kim and I stepped up on the rock ledge above the lake and stood there side by side, facing the sunset. Absolute calm surrounded us. Saturated us. Swallowed us whole. Complete and utter stillness. Not a whisper of noise. The lake a perfect mirror of the mountain above it. The sun setting into a horizon of impossible pastels, painted by the very finger of God. We stood there awestruck, but spent and shaken.

Passed in silence, that moment of Kim and me standing together, shoulder to shoulder, turning our faces toward the warming Sun was truly quickening, and for the very first time I could see in the selfsame sky both my deepest fear and my fondest joy.

Chris Dahl and his wife Kim put their roots down in Western Montana over 30 years ago, the past 20 in the tiny no-stop-light town of Drummond. They raised their four children under the Big Sky, and so far all four kids and their spouses have stayed close and are raising their nine grandkids in the shadows of the mountains of Montana. Chris and Kim started Dahl Wholesale in 1993, a wholesale distribution business selling packaging and shipping supplies, and which is continuing to feed them to this day. They are in a perpetual state of wanderlust and their travels have taken them to Alaska lots of times, Africa twice, New Zealand, Ukraine, Mexico, the Caribbean, Sweden, Israel, Jordan, Egypt, and most recently Tahiti – and Chris usually tries to find something to hunt or fish along the way. They are active in their faith and community, and despite all their travels have never found a place quite like home. Chris grew up in the Snake River plain of Southeastern Idaho, played football for Ricks College back in the day, and graduated from Brigham Young

University in 1987. He says the day after college graduation was one of the best days of his life, all packed up with Kim and baby Devin and seeing Salt Lake City in the rear view mirror headed north! As a youngster, Chris started out after ducks and pheasants with a single shot .410, graduated to rifle hunting for big game, discovered elk hunting in his twenties, suffered through a trophy mule deer buck phase, and most recently has been a dedicated archery snob. His stories have been published in Montana Outdoors, Eastman's Hunting Journal, Real Hunting Magazine, Bugle Magazine, and Bowhunter Magazine. "Lessons From the Mountains" is his first book of non-fiction."